SUMMONING TABLETS OF GUILDS IN HUNGARY

Péter Nagybákay

SUMMONING TABLETS OF GUILDS IN HUNGARY

Corvina Kiadó

Title of the original: Magyarországi céhbehívótáblák
Corvina Kiadó, Budapest, 1981

Translated by Susan Horn
Translation revised by Elisabeth West
Design by Erzsébet Szabados
Map and text illustrations by Zsuzsa Erdélyi
Photographs by
Oszkár Hernádi: 23a–b, 27, 41a—b
Levente Szepsi Szűcs: 10a, 11a–d, 12a–b, 15a–b, 24, 26a–b, 37a–b, 42a
János Szerencsés: 34, 48
Jászberény Museum: 8a–b
Béla Hegede: all the other black-and-white and colour plates

On the jacket: Painted hardwood summoning tablet of the Szekszárd boot-makers' guild (1766).
Museum of Applied Arts, Budapest
On the back of jacket: Summoning tablet
of the Csongrád carpenters' and millers' guild (early 19th century)

ISBN 963 13 1066 3
Printed in Hungary, 1981
Révai Printing House,
CO1972-h-8185

The Development of the Guild System, Its Administration and Surviving Relics

The guild system—the organized form of the artisan industry throughout Europe—was prevalent in Hungary for over five hundred years. Many different views have been advanced as to the origin and development of the system in Hungary. However, one thing is beyond doubt—that although it was possibly modelled on the Roman and Byzantine systems, its establishment was closely connected with the division of labour and the development of towns resulting from economic and social progress in Western Europe after the migration period.

Guilds were first developed to protect the interests of men plying the same craft within a given area, the prime objective being to ensure for the members exclusive rights and privileges on the local market. By concentrating on this aim the guilds of feudal Hungary became powerful and exclusive organizations with an influence that extended beyond the boundaries of the country. They also contributed greatly to cultural development. Additional significance was given to the system when itinerant journeymen began to pass on new techniques and so raise the general level of achievement.

The first guilds were formed in Italy and Flanders, in the medieval towns where labour, trade and industry were first organized. These guilds acquired great prestige, gradually assuming responsibility for the protection and administration of the towns. In many places they organized revolts against outside feudal powers which threatened their own autonomy; also against the local patricians, for instance in Florence and Gand.

In Hungary too the guild system originated in the most advanced towns: Esztergom, Buda and Pest, and presumably also in Székesfehérvár, where they can be traced back to the thirteenth century. In these towns the merchants and craftsmen—who probably came originally from Venice, Lombardy or the Frankish regions beyond the Rhine and were collectively called "the Latins"—inhabited separate districts, self-governed and with their own privileges. By the fourteenth century Flemish, Lower-Rhenish and Westphalian *hospes* or guest settlers, collectively known as "Italians" and "Saxons", were living in Transylvania and the Szepesség, also in other parts of Upper Hungary, including the towns of Pozsony, Kassa and even Debrecen. Here they began to develop a means of protecting the interests of the craftsmen. They abolished competition and freed themselves from the authority of the landowners, but not without strictly complying to the religious formalities required in the Middle Ages when the Church was all-powerful. First they acquired a monopoly to purchase raw material and sell finished products. This was followed by the institution of guild rules based on an acceptance of the practical advantages inherent in interdependence, the protection of common interests and organization. Similar developments were uniformly inaugurated all over Europe. It was a gradual process effected when local economic and social conditions seemed favourable. In Hungary the most extensive organization of the guilds took place in the fifteenth century.

We can assume that the guilds were modelled on the ancient "neighbourhood" *(Nachbarschaft)* associations already in existence in Flanders, Westphalia and the Lower-Rhenish region, also the religious bodies formed for the care of certain altars. This heritage of constitutional structures and regulations remained most influential among the Transylvanian Saxons. The guilds, however, formulated more positive and accurately defined economic aims. One justification of this assumption is the fact that craftsmen plying the same trade usually lived in one particular street. There are, however, theories to the contrary, namely that it was when the simpler "neighbourhood" associations combined as a result of agricultural settlements that they adopted the advanced organizational statutes and solemn ceremonies characteristic of the guilds. This sphere of influence of the guilds is clearly recognizable in the young farmers' societies, shepherds' guilds and associations for vineyard-owners.

It is now almost impossible to trace the way in which the guilds were originally organized and the evolution of the guild system. The precursors of the guilds—both "neighbourhood" and religious groups—were similarly organized and the ceremonies associated with them were almost identical.

The development of the Hungarian guilds differed in many respects from the general pattern of development in Western Europe; urban growth was also different and came later than in the western part of the Continent. While the Hungarian guild system was being reorganized after the Turkish occupation, the guilds in Western Europe, powerful, distinguished and rich, had already lost much of their economic significance; some of them had even ceased to function, for their very existence was incompatible with the free competition of early capitalism. It was quite otherwise in Hungary where there was a revitalization of the guilds in market-towns and villages even as late as during the first decades of the nineteenth century. True, these developments were modest and unassuming compared to what had been seen in the West, for the simple reason that the majority of the guild members, including the masters, were engaged in agricultural work during part of the year, and their living conditions hardly differed from those of the peasants with whom they closely shared both work and social activities.

The guild was an exclusive body that functioned according to definite rules, its sphere of activity and economic interests being determined and ensured by charter granted by the feudal state. The rules of the guilds limited internal and external competition, and regulated in detail the quality of the products, moral attitudes, methods of training, the legal position of the apprentices, journeymen and masters, the members' religious duties, their obligations to help each other and to support orphans, widows and the sick, and finally their tasks connected with funerals, fire-fighting and the defence of the town.

Each guild was headed by one or more guild-masters elected by the members for a period of one year. It was the duty of the guild-master—or chief guild-master if there were more than one—to convene the ordinary and extraordinary meetings, to direct the corporate body and ensure that all guild regulations were observed. He also exercised certain judiciary rights and was authorized to impose punishments.

The acting guild-master guarded the chest containing not only the charter, documents and seal of the guild but also the accumulated fees of the members, any fines, and all valuable assets. The chest was always opened with great ceremony and the meetings were held around it. The guild-master was also in charge of the vessels used at banquets held in celebration of important events—as for instance the initiation of a journeyman or a master. These vessels comprised jugs, cups, goblets (called *billikom* in Hungarian, a distortion of the German *Willkomm*, meaning welcome), plates and dishes. The guild-master was also responsible for the safekeeping of the guild's portable emblem of supremacy, the summoning tablet.

The Function of Summoning Tablets in Hungary

The summoning tablet was the symbol of the guild's authority. It was by circulating this object that the guild-master summoned members to meetings. In the Hungarian literature it is called *behívótábla* (summoning tablet) precisely because of its use; it should be noted, however, that this word is not mentioned in contemporary sources nor does it appear on the objects themselves. The united guild of Miskolc was probably the only organization with a tablet, made in 1812, with the inscription *Einladungs Zeichen* (invitation sign). It has sometimes been described as *bemondótábla* (announcer's tablet), especially if no written message was attached to it. Many tablets were provided with a small box to contain—or a band to hold fast—a document, and it was the bearer's task to read out the guild-masters's message. In such cases he presented the tablet and "announced" the communication. There is a reference dated 1741 in which the summoning tablet of the Buda butchers' guild is called *Einsag* (announcer). At the Hungarian millennial exhibition in 1896, the thousandth anniversary of the Hungarian Conquest, a group of guild tablets were labelled "guild bearers' tablets". There are several references to the "carrying of the tablet", as in the regulations of the knife-makers' guild, dating from 1674. In 1905 F. Rómer, archaeologist and historian used the name *meghívó tábla* (invitation tablet). The tablet of the Nagyatád (Somogy County) weavers was listed in an inventory of 1907 as *beparancsoló tábla* (summoning or order tablet).

Nowadays, in modern Hungarian literature we generally find the simple designation *tábla* (tablet) or *céh táblája* (guild tablet). The tablet of the boot-makers' guild at Csákvár (Fejér County) bears the inscription *járató tábla* (errand tablet), while for the same object the furriers of Kézdivásárhely employ in their documents the term *kerülőtábla* (tablet for the rounds). In Eger and Debrecen the literature refers to *hirdető tábla* (notice tablet), and in Rozsnyó a *halotti hirdető táblácska* (death notice tablet) was circulated to call guild members to vigils and funerals. On other occasions the guild tablet in Rozsnyó was called *jel* (sign) or *céh jel* (guild sign), which designation occurred also in Jolsva, Miskolc and Debrecen. In an invitation dated 1922 to the tanners of Miskolc there is a reference to the tablet as *közjel* (community sign). In Sáros County the guild signs were called *künnjáró jel* (dispatch sign).

The designation evidently derives from a literal translation of the Latin *insigne* or *signum*, or it may be a translation of the German *Zeichen*, for the German word used in

Hungary for the summoning tablet was generally *Zeichen* or *Zunftzeichen*, though in Transylvania the name *Tafel* or *Tafelt* occurs in some documents. In Latin the summoning tablet is often referred to as *tabula*. In Croatian it is *tablica;* in the Slovak literature it is recorded as *zvolácia tabulka*, and in the Rumanian as *tabla de breasla, tabla breslei* or *tabla umblatoare*.

Members of a guild could be summoned to meet for several purposes. There were regular quarterly meetings and monthly or weekly meetings at which the masters discussed matters of common interest and made essential decisions, for instance, with regard to elections. Meetings were also convened after the death of a member or to discuss problems of individual members; but in such cases a special fee was charged to the interested party for the circulation of the summoning tablet. In the knife-makers' guild of Debrecen the tablet had to be sent round to convene a meeting if a new journeyman was to be admitted into the guild and also if a member wished to take up a different craft. For this the journeyman had to pay 12 coins. Every journeyman of the coopers' guild in Miskolc (1674) had to ask for meeting of the guild at the start and at the completion of his masterwork (his examination for mastership). We also know from a case that came before the Kassa Council (1666) that the barbers, who originally acted also as surgeons, had to have the guild tablet circulated before performing a major surgical operation. Only after holding what might be called a consultation with the assembled guild members could he embark upon the operation.

Members were summoned to meetings by circulating the summoning tablet. This procedure was described as the "circulation of the tablet", an expression still in use in the nineteenth and twentieth centuries. The same expression was used in the charter of incorporation issued to the Debrecen tailors in 1468, a document which was transcribed literally and confirmed by King John in 1530; the Hungarian translation dates from the beginning of the seventeenth century. The oldest charters issued in Transylvania and some of the Upper Hungarian regions including the Szepesség in the fifteenth century contained the expressions *Wenn man das Zeichen umgetragen* (Segesvár, 1484), *umschickt* (Bártfa, 1499), *umsendet wird* (Késmárk, 1515), *herumbgehet* (Lőcse, 1518) —all of which convey the notion of "circulation". From that time on the Hungarian expression *táblajáratás* (circulation of the tablet) has been in constant use without any change in the meaning until the middle of the twentieth century; it is found in

guild charters of incorporation, minutes of meetings and other documents and also persists in the oral idiom throughout Hungary and Transylvania.
The summoning tablet was sent out by the guild-master. For this procedure there were also several expressions.
The circulating of a tablet with the armorial sign—the means of communicating official messages to members—was effected in two different ways.
Sometimes the tablet was taken round by a functionary of the guild, usually the "master-in-waiting". This office was held by the youngest master of the guild, being passed on whenever a master younger than himself was admitted. The master-in-waiting was therefore known as the "junior master" in many places. His official duties were arduous, as he was generally responsible for all field-work which he had to carry out or risk severe punishment. In Rozsnyó, Somorja and Sárospatak the tablet was taken round by the "visiting master". In many places attendance at a guild meeting was also called "visiting". In the tailors' guild in Nagyszombat the visiting master, who had to perform the strenuous task of carrying the tablet round, was simply called "the master of the tablet". Here this office was held by each member in turn, but those who could avoid it, did so, though naturally they had to pay for the exemption. Carrying round the tablet was particularly tiring when members lived at a considerable distance from each other—a not infrequent state of affairs, especially in the provinces.
Another way of circulating the tablet was for the masters to share the task, each master passing on the tablet with its message to his nearest fellow-member either personally or by sending his journeyman or apprentice. Hence the expression *tablet neighbour* used by the Debrecen tanners. Each member continued to pass on the tablet in the same way, according to a definite predetermined order of precedence which was not to be broken. Finally the tablet had to be returned in good order to the guild-master who had originally sent it on its rounds. The Debrecen fullers had a special name for the last master in the chain—the one who returned the tablet to the guild-master. They called him "the son of the tablet".
Regulation VI of the statutes of the Debrecen knife-makers' guild, issued in 1674, offers clear proof of how carefully the members watched over the punctual and conscientious forwarding of the tablet: "Let any one of the master knife-makers carry the guild tablet without care; let him rest it on the floor, leave it unguarded on a window-

sill or lose it, then shall a fine of two florins be imposed on him; nor shall any knife-maker journeyman be exempt from his obligation to carry round the tablet; should any journeyman fail in this, then shall he be subject to a fine of twenty-five coins." The seriousness of the procedure and the respect shown to the tablet as a symbol of guild authority is reflected also by the fact that when it was the master who carried the tablet to his nearest fellow-member he presented himself clean, tidy and wearing clothes usually reserved for Sundays. Traces of this tradition still lingered at Gönc (Abaúj County) in 1957. If a message was sent by word of mouth, great care was taken that it should be accurately transmitted without any distortion. For instance the rules of the oldest Transylvanian Saxon guild stipulate that anyone "distorting the sign" *(das Verdrehen des Zeichens)* that is, transmitting a message inaccurately, conveying anything other than the original meaning, would be liable to punishment.

It was, of course, extremely important that the circulation of the guild tablet should take place speedily, so that messages might reach members of the guild before the day was out. The care that was shown in this matter is evidenced in the nineteenth and twentieth-century written messages, sent in a small box attached to the tablets, which usually ended with the words "to be passed on urgently" or "to be carried in all haste". Similarly, from as early as the fifteenth century the guild charters stipulated that severe punishment would be meted out to anyone who retained the guild tablet overnight. There is for example a regulation to this effect in the 1484 charter of the Segesvár furriers' guild. The Munkács tanners were instructed to stop working the moment they received the guild tablet and to pass it on without delay.

In the case of large guilds or where masters lived at a considerable distance from each other, several summoning tablets were sent round. These were dispatched simultaneously but in different directions. Thus the Szatmárnémeti and Debrecen boot-makers used six almost identical tablets, and in 1855 the Miskolc boot-makers had four new ones made to add to those they already possessed. This was necessary, as the guild of boot-makers had the largest membership. At one count, during the first half of the nineteenth century, the number of master boot-makers exceeded 750 in Debrecen and 600 in Miskolc. The Miskolc tailors also used four summoning tablets. The Veszprém millers circulated two almost exactly identical tablets, each one marked with the date 1797, as the distance between the mills on the rivers was very great and it would not have been possible to summon members to an urgent meeting by means of only one tablet. The joint rules of the millers of Abaúj-Zemplén-Borsod and Gömör Counties contain provisions dating from 1670 to ensure that the guild-master would be informed of the death of any member. It was then his duty to circulate the guild tablet, assemble members from the neighbourhood and arrange a decent burial for the deceased member.

One of the essential conditions for the effective functioning of a guild was the rallying of the members. Any master who failed to appear at a meeting and was unable to give an acceptable excuse for his absence was therefore severely punished, the essential concern of the guilds from their earliest beginnings being to protect the common interests of all the members. It was laid down in the regulations of the Debrecen furriers, dated 1449, that a fine of four Hungarian pints (about twelve English pints) of wine was to be imposed on any member who failed to appear when summoned by the guild-master. According to the regulations of the Veszprém tanners dated 1692, a member who failed to be present at a meeting announced by means of the guild tablet was to be fined one florin on the first occasion, a further florin on the second occasion, and four florins if the offence was repeated a third time. The Szenic (Nyitra County) button-braiders were even more severe, for their guild-master was entitled to seize something as security from the defaulting member and was even allowed to call in the constable should he need assistance in carrying out his orders.

Failure to circulate the tablet, or to appear at the guild-master's election, could as a last resort incur a suspension of the rights of the defaulting member. There is for instance an interesting case concerning a master boot-maker of Kassa, recorded in a document dated 1663. The relevant passage runs as follows: "István Pásztor having failed to take delivery of the tablet of the honourable guild and to appear at the hour indicated for the casting of his *vox* (vote) at the election of the guild-master, and he having *contumaciter* (obdurately) failed in his duty to other guild members, the latter will from this day on deprive him of his right to carry the guild tablet until he acts according to the rules."

A summary of the function of the summoning tablet was sometimes engraved on the tablet itself. On one side of the Rimaszombat butchers' guild tablet dating from 1803 there is the following inscription: IMHOL A NEMES MÉSZÁROS CÉNEK TÁB-

LÁJA MINDEN MESTEREMBER CZÉHMESTER ÚR HÁZÁNÁL MEGJELENNYEN 2, FR: BÜNTETÉS (Behold the tablet of the noble Butchers' Guild every master-butcher to appear at the guild-master's house under penalty of 2 Fl.).

A similar inscription can be found on the tablet of the Szekszárd boot-makers: A KÖZÖNSÉGES SEXARDI BÖTSÜLETES CSISMAZIA CZÉHNEK TÁBLÁJA MELLY ÁLTAL MINDEN CZÉHBELI MESTEREK BIZONYOS ÓRAKOR AZ ELRENDELT HELYEN MEGJELENNI PARANNTSOLTATNAK BÜNTETÉS ALATT KÖTELESZTETNEK 1766 (This tablet of the common honourable guild of Szekszárd Boot-makers bids all masters of the guild to appear at the hour and place stated, under pain of penalty 1766).

The tablet of the Miskolc tailors' guild bears the text: AZ MISKOLCZI B. N. SZABÓ CZHÉ TÁBLÁJA ÉPÍTTETET CSETNEKI SZABÓ GYÖRGY FŐ CZHÉ MESTER IDEJÉBEN ÉS FILEKI SZABÓ ISTVÁN KIS CZHÉ MESTERSÉGÉBEN AZ ENGEDELMESEKK ÖRÖMÖKRE, AZ ENGEDETLENEKK BÜNTETÉSEKRE. ANNO DOMINI 1733 die 10 DIK MARTY (The tablet of the honorable and noble Tailors' Guild of Miskolc, built in the time of chief guild-master György Csetncki Szabó and assistant guild-master István Fileki Szabó. Pleasure to the obedient and punishment to those disobedient. March 10. A.D. 1733).

The Ways of Circulating the Tablet

We may summarize the function of the summoning tablet by saying that the tablet was the visible symbol of the authority of the guild enabling the bearer to prove beyond doubt that any message or instruction he might deliver—originally by word of mouth, later in writing—was indeed official and authorized by the head of the organization, the guild-master.

This was particularly necessary in the early medieval period when simple illiterate people were accustomed to the acquisition of knowledge from pictures and symbols. However, the significance of the tablet persisted almost unchanged in later periods of more widespread literacy. Even today we do not consider a document to be official and authentic unless it bears an official seal or stamp.

Thus the role of the summoning tablet was essentially the same as that of the "summoning seal", another device to prove the authenticity of a message or order. In Hungary, in medieval times it was jurisdictional practice for a king's messenger to present the royal seal or ring. However, a round summoning seal 6 cm in diameter (the *billog*, as it was called in old Hungarian) specially cast in bronze and provided with a loop for ease of handling has come down to us from as early as the reign of King Andrew I (1047–1060). The seal bears a likeness of the king enthroned, and is inscribed with his name. The government official entrusted with the summoning seal wore it on a cord round his neck and it was by producing this sign of authority that he summoned the person concerned to appear before the king. In the eleventh century the canon of Veszprém, who also had to act as notary public and judge, wore a metal summoning seal similar to that described above but bearing a likeness of his patron saint, Archangel Michael. French jurisdiction followed the same practice. In France the task of summoning members fell to the clerk of the court known as the *sigillifer* (bearer of the seal), because, like the Hungarian official (the *billogos*), he wore a summoning seal on his chest. And, like the summoning tablet of the guilds, so too the summoning or judicial seal was but a badge of identification, a sign that the bearer was officiall ayuthorized, it was in fact a personal emblem like a coat of arms. Thus the summoning seal is very much akin to the guild tablet, with the difference, however, that the main purpose of the latter—at least in Hungary—was to notify members of meetings or funerals rather than to summon offenders to receive judgment.

This ancient custom of circulating summoning tablets was also prevalent apart from

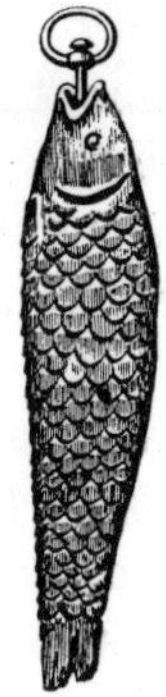

1. Funeral tablet from Bánffyhunyad (1865). In: Dezső Malonyay. *A magyar nép művészete I.* [Hungarian Folk Art I.]. p. 257
2. Summoning badge of the Keszthely fishermen's guild (1859). Balaton Museum, Keszthely

the guilds. At Kalotaszeg and Bánffyhunyad, for example, the office of "street magistrate" was filled by a different person each year and—as Malonyay tells us in his work on Hungarian folk art (1906)—it was the man in office who was in charge of the town's two "funeral tablets". Whenever a funeral was to take place, he dispatched the two tablets early in the morning, one to the right, the other to the left, and the neighbours passed them on to each other with the messages customary on such occasions. The shape and dimensions of the funeral tablet correspond exactly to those of the summoning tablets shaped like hand-mirrors used by guilds in Transylvania, the Partium and Trans-Tisza region (Ill. 1). They were also called *dékány tablets* (from the Latin *decanus*=dean tablets) and in many districts members were invited to attend presbyterial meetings by the same means, that is by circulating the tablet.

There are clear indications that the Saxon neighbourhood *(Nachbarschaft)* associations, mentioned earlier, were characterized by the same organizational structure, customs and forms of ceremony as the guilds. The dimensions, workmanship, form and use of their summoning tablets *(Nachbarschaftzeichen)* were similar to those of the guilds. They are usually shaped like a shield or a heart. Some of the finest pieces among them are several hundred years old. A large number of summoning tablets which once belonged to neighbourhood associations are now in museums at Nagyszeben, Segesvár and Kolozsvár. These associations are generally called *Nachbarschaft* or *Altschaft* in the inscriptions on the tablets, but some tablets mention the old "ten-member" and "hundred-member" associations, known also in Hungary. Thus a wooden summoning tablet dating from 1700 and now in Segesvár is carved with the words *100 Mann Zeichen* (Sign of the 100 Men).

The summoning tablets of the Hungarian guilds were not always made of wood, sometimes they were made of metal, and they were fashioned in various shapes. The tablet was provided with a ring or a handle, and the face was usually decorated with the arms of the guild. In some districts, however, a different type of sign was used, as for example a decorative but characteristic tool, instrument or product of the craft. Thus the boot-makers naturally used the last. This is clearly indicated in the 1583 regulations of the Nyitra boot-makers: "When the guild-master sends round the last or tablet to his fellow-members and it happens that a master is not found at home, and is informed of the circulation of the tablet or the last through his servant, yet fails to appear at the Guild, he shall be subject to a fine of one pound of wax." The custom of sending round a last was also prevalent among the boot-makers of Sopron. The guild-master of the Németprόna cloth-makers sent round an ornate bobbin to summon the masters, while a fish carved in wood served the same purpose among the Keszthely fishermen (Ill. 2).

However, the use of this type of sign was generally confined to journeymen's associations or "small societies" functioning within the guilds under the leadership of a few senior journeymen or "old boys" *(Altgeselle)* elected by the members. They held meetings of their own round their own chest under the supervision of an elderly "past master" appointed for the purpose. The senior journeymen of the Németpróna boot-makers sent round a small wooden boot covered with black leather to summon the young men to a funeral or meeting. The "dean" of the Érsekújvár barbers "wanting to assemble the journeymen circulated a razor" (1743).

However, in the case of journeymen's associations it was the key of the chest that was most often circulated to convene a meeting. This is one indication that they possessed neither a tablet nor a seal and were not authorized to wear a special badge or use a coat of arms. The key of the chest was a substitute for such emblems. In the journeymen's associations or "small societies" circulating the key or dispatching the key had the same significance as the tablet in the "masters' guilds". The Miskolc furrier journeymen dispatched the key, the Vác journeymen carried it, the Székesfehérvár and Kőszeg boot-maker journeymen circulated it, while among the journeymen's associations in Veszprém County the term generally used was to issue the key.

3. Summoning key of the Kolozsvár association of young master tailors. Museum of History, Kolozsvár
4. Ferule with list of members of the cape-makers' guild in Miskolc (19th century). Herman Ottó Museum, Miskolc

In Kolozsvár, where in 1678 the tailors' guild introduced separate regulations for the Young Master Tailors' Association, the key used to summon members was ornamented with a crown and a double-eagle, and provided with a handle (Ill. 3). When not in circulation, the key was kept in a silk-lined case by the "key-master" in office. There are also records from Kolozsvár dating from 1554, according to which the "dean" of the tailor journeymen assembled the members by circulating the key.

Finally we have to mention the "most modern" form of summoning tablet, one on which names of members were listed. This was adopted when literacy became more widespread in the second half of the nineteenth century. A paper document with the list of names was attached to a long, narrow wooden tablet with a handle or a triangular or quadrangular rod with a grip. This type of summoning tablet was, in certain respects, the successor of the tablet with a box in which written messages were often placed together with a membership list. In Csongrád County each master put a cross after his name to confirm that he had noted the message.

The tablet or rod with a membership list has, however, much earlier historical associations. It was a symbol of guild authority no less than the guild summoning tablet —usually shield-shaped and bearing the guild coat of arms (as clearly indicated by the tablet of the Rimaszombat butchers' guild on which there is a reference to the coat of arms in the inscription describing the heraldic device on the face). The herald's staff or relay baton were closely akin to the ornamental rod or staff widely used by western guilds and known by various German names (*Stab*, *Aufschlagstab*, *Ordonnanzstab*,

Schafferstab, *Schaffergesellenstab*, *Reglement*). The guild-master or "dean" banged the table with the official rod if a guild-meeting or a journeymen's assembly became too tumultuous. The rod was also the symbol of authority and was used ceremonially to maintain public order; this symbolism was generally recognized. The judge's rod was well known in Hungary and was almost looked upon as the "sceptre of the guild".
For special occasions these ornately carved sticks, reminiscent of sceptres, were adorned with ribbons. For example, the sign of authority of the "past master" of the Németpróna cloth-maker and boot-maker journeymen was called the "rod of justice" (*Gerechtigkeit*, *Lopate* from the Slav word *lopata* or Hungarian *lapát*=spade); on festive occasions this was adorned with ribbons and a bunch of flowers. This was the instrument used to administer 1 to 12 strokes on young lawbreakers. In shape it corresponded to the so-called *ferula* or *ferolle* (ferule) used for summoning guild members in Bohemia, Moravia and Vogtland—an area in the Erzgebirge bordering on Bohemia. There was also a similarity between the rod and the sign of authority called "paddle" or "bat", a disciplinary board with a bored handle used by the leader of the village lads' associations, the lads' judge, associations also widely known in Hungary. Here, too, the instrument was known as the *ferula* (ferule).
There is no doubt that, in view of its intended purpose, the rod counted as an important badge of guild authority, but in Hungary little evidence of the use of such "service rods" (embodying the sceptre) can be found. It would seem that in this country it was the other symbol of power, the tablet representing the coat of arms or shield, that became predominant, and only such summoning tablets provided with a handle and bearing the membership roll show some affinity with the ferules. The earliest extant tablet with a handle showing a list of names is that of the Debrecen coopers, made in 1789, but similar ones had been in use in a number of other places including Pápa, Miskolc (Ill. 4), Munkács, Kolozsvár and Székelyudvarhely. The paper attached usually bears the inscription "list of names", but the Debrecen rope-makers of 1821 called it catalogue, the name still used for the attendance register at universities, while the rod of the tanners (or cordovan workers) of Székelyudvarhely, similarly listing the names of members, fully corresponds to that of the Székelyudvarhely college where it was known as the *apparitor* (attendance rod or janitor's rod). Thus it was the symbol of attendance (presence), maintenance of public order and chastisement.

Guild Badges Used in Europe

Even as recently as the mid-thirties we find, in a Brukenthal Museum publication, a claim made by Dr. Julius Bielz that the use of summoning tablets by craft guilds was scarcely known outside Transylvania. Now, however, we have certain proof that the use of such tablets was customary throughout Hungary, and even in Croatia, a country with a close constitutional relationship with Hungary. Evidence of this may be found in the regulations of the guilds which include specific instructions for the circulation of the summoning tablet. Guild records also include numerous references to the tablets. Finally, a great many tablets have survived while others, though lost, have been described in documents which can still be seen. We know of nearly 500 summoning tablets. When analysed according to territory and craft we find 120 settlements and 40 different crafts. We can therefore be confident that the use of summoning tablets was widespread among the guilds.

It is, therefore, surprising that in the extensive German literature on guilds there is practically no mention at all of summoning tablets in references to surviving treasures of the guilds, whether of artistic or material value. German scholars have described innumerable seals, chests, vessels, flags, funeral arms, torches and other ritual objects used by the guilds, but they give scarcely any information about the summoning tablet, especially in relation to mid- and south German territories. Nor was the tablet known in Austria. The authoritative study of guild signs published by Leopold Schmidt, the well-known ethnographer, in 1973, mentions only one single tablet from the Austrian collections, and that comes from East Silesia. It is called *Ladetafel* (invitation tablet) and was used in Jablunka, a village in a Polish-speaking area close to the old Hungarian border. We also know from the regulations of the cloth-makers of Bielsko near Jablunka in East Silesia, that instructions for carrying round the guild badge were in exactly the same form as those used in the charters of the guilds in Upper Hungary.

Although the custom of summoning the members by circulating a guild symbol was also prevalent in Bohemia, Moravia and Vogtland (Erzgebirge), it was not a tablet that was used but the so-called *ferula*, the ornamental sceptre with the guild coat of arms.

Scattered traces of the use of summoning tablets can be found in northern Bohemia near the borders of Silesia, or, to be more accurate, the former territory of Lusica.

Here the tablet was called *Ladebrett* (invitation tablet) or *Gebotebrett* (order tablet) and—as among the Transylvanian Saxons—it was used by the municipal administration as well as by the guilds. In the Municipal Museum of Meissen (Saxony), near Bohemia and Lusica, there is a tin sign bearing a design of rope-laying tools and with the date 1748 which, judging by its shape and size, must certainly have served as a summoning tablet.

The search for documentary evidence and the remains of guild tablets and badges now leads us towards north-west Germany. In a work dealing with rules for journeymen, published in Magdeburg in 1844, we are told that meetings, especially "meetings extraordinary" were announced to the smiths by means of a nail or a hammer, and to boot-makers by the key of the guild chest. The cartouche-shaped summoning emblem made in 1623 and used by the Stralsund shipwrights is now in the Stralsund Museum of History. However, Karl Gröber, in his authoritative study of the splendid collection of guild relics associated with all the German-speaking territories, mentions only one single summoning tablet in his list of treasures once owned by guilds, namely the *Botenschild* (herald's shield) of the Bremen sailors dating from 1718. It is a small silver badge which the *Bote* (herald) of the corporate body wore pinned to his coat when making his rounds. It is decorated with a design showing two sailors with various nautical instruments. Numerous other summoning badges are now in Bremen in the Focke Museum, among them that of the masons dating from 1764 (Ill. 5), and the carpenters dating from 1766.

Records of the Bremen guilds supply accurate information on the regular circulation of their summoning tablets. In her work on medieval Bremen guilds, Elisabeth Thikötter has described in detail how the chief and assistant guild-masters were helped by messengers or heralds *(Bote)*. The duties of the latter were always performed by the youngest guild member, as in Hungary where they fell to the junior master (Bremen turners, 1661). Later some of the guilds (the Bremen boot-makers, for example) entrusted to special paid employees some of the more arduous tasks, since these were found to absorb time otherwise devoted to production. In the late fifteenth century the regulations of the Bremen tailors' guild *(Botenordnung)* limited the number of heralds to four. At that time a herald was still counted as an important official and it was an honour to act as such.

5. Summoning tablet of the Bremen masons' guild (1764). Focke Museum, Bremen

The Münster Landesmuseum also houses several small seventeenth and eighteenth-century summoning shields *(Botenschild)* which were once used by different Münster craft guilds or *Bruderschaft* (brotherhood) associations.

The heralds and couriers played an important role in the Middle Ages. The duties of royal and papal envoys, and the shield-bearing heralds of the nobles, were essentially the same as those of the messengers associated with churches, monasteries, universities, towns and merchant and craft guilds, namely the carrying and transmission of official messages. The heralds generally set out on a long journey with a stick called *Botenspieß* or *Botenstab* (herald's spit or herald's baton) and as in a relay, passed on the baton for each stage of the journey. To safeguard their prestige in the eyes of the public the professional heralds dressed in the colours of their masters or wore a small box *(Büchse)*, generally made of silver, and suspended from the left side of their cloaks or hung round their necks; later this was replaced by a small shield-shaped badge (Ill. 6). The origin of the box, pouch or purse-shaped badge is unknown. It is too small to have held a written message; a letter would not have fitted into it; indeed, it was not made to open. Perhaps it symbolized the postman's bag. It is certain, however, that in the fifteenth century it was in use all over Central Europe, only disappearing gradually during the seventeenth century when it was almost exclusively replaced by the shield-shaped badge. We have evidence that these small boxes and shield-shaped heralds' badges were used in Hatting, Soest, Frankfurt-am-Main, Dortmund and Constance. Apart from Westphalia, the small box or pouch-shaped badges worn by the heralds were widely used in the provinces of the Netherlands. This is borne out by the fact that the Dutch word *bodebus* (*Botenbüchse*, herald's box, courier's pouch) was in general use. This term was used for all badges—those worn by royal messengers, couriers of national or local authorities and heralds of craft guilds and other associations; it was used for badges in the original pouch shape and for those in the shape of a shield. Another Dutch name for them was *draagteken* (*Tragezeichen*, portable badge). And so we move now to the Netherlands, the territory bordering on Westphalia.

The most important of the decorative and valuable guild relics once used in the area which now falls within the boundaries of Holland are the summoning badges, a literal translation being: herald's portable pouches *(bodebus)* or portable badges *(draagteken)*. Their function was the same as in Hungary: they served to identify the envoys. These badges worn by the guild heralds *(knechts of boden)* were usually round and were embossed or engraved with symbols of the craft. In 1964, in an exhibition held in the Amsterdam Museum of History, it was possible to see a large number of such summoning badges, among them those of the Nijmegen sailors from the second half of the fifteenth century (Ill. 7), also badges of the weavers' guild from 1587, and an Arnhem butchers' guild from 1616. In 1967 an exhibition illustrating the history of guilds was held in the Municipal and Provincial Museum in Groningen where the exhibits included the cartouche-shaped summoning badge of the Groningen tailors dating from 1645 (Ill. 8), and sailors' badges representing ships dating from 1663 and 1754. The exhibits also included the chest of a merchant guild *(Kremer)* made in 1619 and decorated with a painted representation of the guild herald in full robes with a badge representing a pair of scales on the left front of his short cloak (Ill. 9).

It was not only in Holland that summoning badges were used, but also in Belgium (Gand, Bruges, Liège, Brussels) and in Northern France (Saint-Trond, Hasselt). In the French-speaking countries there was a special name for the messenger who went round summoning guild members to an assembly. He was called the *bedeau* which corresponds to the Dutch *bode*, the German *Bote* and the Hungarian *szolgáló mester*= "master-in-waiting". The name *bedellus* or *pedellus*, used in Hungary for the janitor at universities, derives from the same word, for the duties of the *bedeau*—like those of the "master-in-waiting" or the court orderly—included every task of an office attendant, from door-keeping to the delivery of a summons.

6. Nobleman's herald with shield-shaped herald's badge round his neck.
From a 15th-century Viennese playing card

7. Badge of the Nijmegen (Holland) sailors' guild (15th century). Rijksmuseum, Amsterdam
8. Summoning tablet of the Groningen (Holland) tailors' guild (1640). Municipal and Provincial Museum, Groningen

The nineteenth-century scholar Felix de Vigne has described in detail the organization, customs and badges of the guilds in Belgium and the north of France. The *bedeau*, or "master-in-waiting" and courier of the guild, wore a short jacket, on the breast of which was a badge showing the guild emblem. One of his main duties was to convene the masters and, as in Hungary, he too was liable to a penalty for any negligence in the performance of his duties. Penalties were also imposed on masters who failed to appear when summoned. The cost of the uniform of the "master-in-waiting" was borne by the guild. The guild-masters, and often the jurymen, too, wore silver-gilt badges suspended on a band or chain over their ceremonial robes. This was known in France as an *affiche* or simply *décoration.* Since the literal meaning of *affiche* is "bill" or "notice" and the figurative sense is "an outward sign" or "proof", there is no doubt that similar badges were also worn by the "masters-in-waiting" who called on members to advise them of forthcoming assemblies. It is, therefore, difficult to tell for certain today whether a shield or cartouche-shaped badge was used exclusively as an ornamental badge of authority worn by leading members of a guild, or whether it was also used to convene meetings. We would mention three examples of such badges from Gand: the fishermens' badge with the guild coat of arms depicting three fish and the patron saint, St. Peter; the brewers' badge from 1628 decorated with the brewers' arms and a representation of St. Arnold in pontificals; and the coopers' badge with the customary Christian representation of St. Martin of Tours cutting off a piece of his cloak for a shivering beggar (Ill. 10).

9. Herald of the Groningen merchant guild, wearing a short cloak with summoning badge (1619).
A painting on the guild chest. Municipal and Provincial Museum, Groningen

As may be seen from the above, the Hungarian custom of circulating the summoning tablet can be clearly traced through Silesia, Lusica, Saxony, Westphalia and Holland as far as Flanders, that felicitous melting pot of Latin and Germanic cultures. It was there, through the guilds, under the leadership of a Gand master brewer, Jakob Arteveld, that the bourgeoisie first acquired power in the middle of the fourteenth century.

However, traces of summoning tablets can be found also in Italy, the second most developed country, economically and socially, in medieval Europe. The Italian *hospes* who settled in Hungary very early assimilated the language of their new homeland so that their origin and the route by which they arrived here are practically unknown. Nevertheless, as there was a link between the Italians and the Angevins and as the guilds were first centrally organized by King Louis the Great of Hungary, it is quite conceivable that the administrative structure of the guilds and some of their customs derived from the Italian system. There may also have been parallel influences at work, since the Italian guilds maintained direct relations with Flanders. The summoning tablet of the Florentine wool-weavers' guild is known to us; this guild had agents who were very active in the trading communities of Bruges in Flanders, also Venice, Paris and London. The Florentine guild wool-weavers belonged to the group of seven distinguished corporations which from the middle of the thirteenth century was able to assume a major role in local government. The *universitas artis lanae* or *Arte della Lana*, the statutes, that is, of the wool-weavers' guild, recognized the office of the *nuntius* or herald and supervised his appointment, his duties and his remuneration. The *nuntius* was one of the important officers responsible to the "university" of masters, and summoning the guild members represented one of his main duties. The summoning tablet of the guild, a small shield believed to be the earliest surviving example of its kind, is now in the Museo Nazionale in Florence. It dates from the fourteenth century, a fine example of Florentine art, about 25 cm in height. The Norman shield, concave and almond-shaped, is enamelled in darkest blue and decorated with heraldic figures made of metal: in the centre a halved lamb looking backwards to the left, the right fore-foot grasping a flag bearing the cross; the rod to which the flag is attached ends in a cross. It is a typical Christian representation of *Agnus Dei* as well as a meaningful symbol of this particular craft. Above the lamb there is a row of four stylized heraldic

10. Summoning tablet of the Gand (Belgium) coopers' guild (17th century). From Félix de Vigne's book on the craft guilds of Belgium and northern France (Gand, 1857)
11. Summoning tablet of the Florentine wool-weavers' guild (14th century). National Museum, Florence

lilies from the coat of arms of the city of Florence. The two centre lilies are surrounded by an inscription. This shield-shaped badge was probably worn by the heralds in their belts and the letter to be delivered could have been carried in the hollow part of the concave shield (Ill. 11).

The widespread use of the summoning tablet and especially the early evidence found in Hungary concerning the custom of circulating it — indisputable evidence can be found in the "Saxon" towns of Transylvania, the Szepesség, and towns inhabited at one time by foreign, western *hospes*, Italian by origin, as for example Nagyvárad and Debrecen — leads us to conclude that the Hungarian guilds adopted an organizational system developed by the earliest known guilds, those of Flanders and Italy. It is possible that the custom was prevalent at some time in central and southern Germany, but, if so, it must have died out there at an early date, while in Hungary it became so firmly established that it might well seem to have been unique to our country. In the sixteenth and seventeenth centuries this ancient custom had been adopted by most of the guilds which were at that time assuming markedly Magyar characteristics, while later, after the end of the Turkish rule, it struck root also among the guilds re-established in the liberated territories (Map, Ill. 12). It will be found, however, that this applies primarily to guilds which were Hungarian in character or which had ties with Transylvania or Upper Hungary. That is, territories not occupied by the Turks. The new guilds formed by south German and Austrian settlers seldom used the summoning tablet. Thus although many decorative relics have come down to us from the guilds of Buda, Pest and Szeged, these include scarcely any such tablets, nor do we know of a

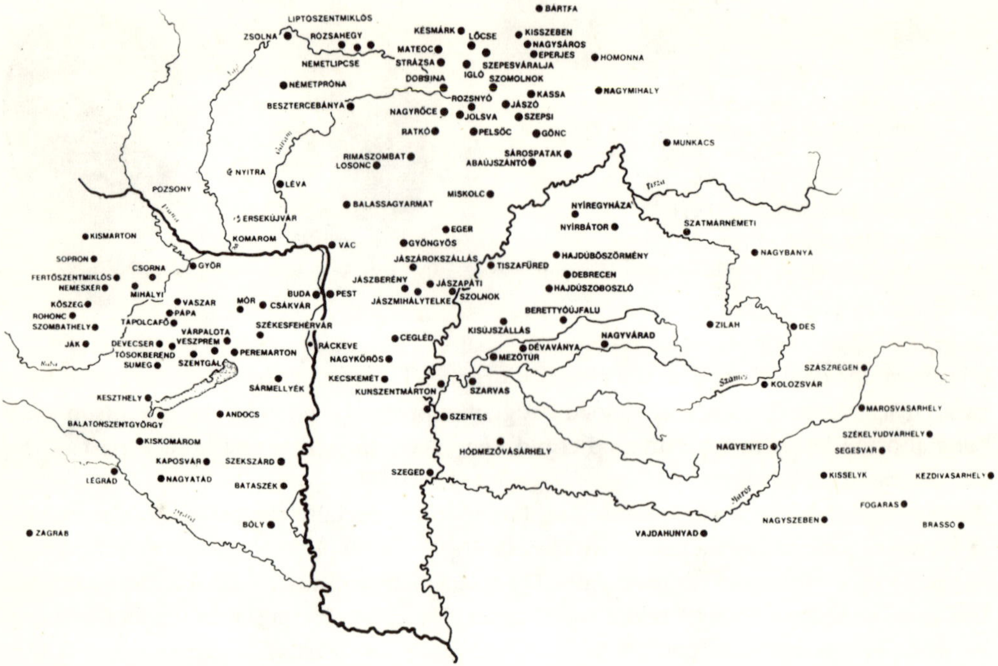

12. The spread of the use of guild summoning tablets in historical Hungary

single one from Pécs. However, there are still in existence numerous summoning tablets from Veszprém County, Kecskemét, Nagykőrös, Szentes and Hódmezővásárhely, and an almost complete series from Miskolc and Debrecen. As for those counties near the Austrian border, which were not subjugated by the Turks and where there was therefore no break in the continuity of the guilds—possibly because they remained strongly influenced by the Austrians—the number of summoning tablets found in these areas is considerably less. The tablets that do exist were used by guilds specifically Hungarian in character (as for example the Kőszeg and Szombathely button-braiders' guild, the Ják potters' guild and the Nemeskér boot-makers' guild).

Types of Summoning Tablets

About 500 summoning tablets of guilds within the former territories of Hungary, including Transylvania and Croatia, are known to us. Most of them are now in museums, a few in private collections. Some of them are made of metal: copper, tin or silver; but most are carved of wood and often have painted decorations. The majority of the wooden tablets are of pear, walnut or beech-wood, and some are embellished with an inlaid pattern of wood or bone. The earthenware and leather-covered pieces are rare. The size of the tablets depends to some extent on the material they are made of. The metal ones are generally small, measuring 13 cm to 20 cm in height, and 8 cm to 15 cm in width; the wooden ones are somewhat larger: 18 cm to 28 cm high and 14 cm to 20 cm wide (without handle). In Upper Hungary—a territory rich in metal—copper tablets were the more widespread, while in Transylvania wooden ones were more usual. In other parts of the country, tablets were made of both wood and metal as locally available. It is noticeable, however, that it is the older tablets that are made of carved wood, the more recent ones of copper. When compared with the summoning tablets that have survived in north Germany, Holland and Begium—most of which are the work of silversmiths—the Hungarian tablets are seen to be more modest, even as to basic material. This can be readily understood if we consider that the Hungarian guilds had none of the political and economic power wielded by guilds in the more developed western European countries.

Nevertheless, in view of the strikingly large number and nationwide use of summoning tablets among guilds in Hungary—for it must be borne in mind that their use had become traditional in the simplest village guilds—it is necessary to analyse these characteristically Hungarian badges as examples of handicraft, folk art, heraldry, iconography; we must also study the techniques involved in making them—in fact, the whole range of their cultural and historical significance.

The tablets discussed in this book—140 in all—were made over a period spanning nearly four centuries. They were made and shaped for a specific function. When they were first made total illiteracy necessitated the transmission of messages by word of mouth rather than in writing. It is from that early period that most of the shield-shaped tablets originate. They were circulated purely as the emblem or coat of arms of the guild. The heralds sometimes wore them suspended round their necks; sometimes they merely held up the tablet for all to see. Already it is clear that they were closely related to the royal or ecclesiastical summoning seals described earlier. The period when the summoning tablets were still made without a cavity to contain a written message may be designated as the period of "announcing" boards.

When written messages came into use they were fastened to one side of the tablet with sealing wax. Later a band was riveted to the tablet or a small case with a copper door attached to it to hold the written message. From this time on the tablet assumed a different function. This new type of tablet was from the outset made with a case to hold a document. The shield form became less frequent and was superseded by small cases, architectural in their structure and ornamentation; small suspendable wall-cupboards either for hanging or free-standing; and quite frequently book-shaped caskets or small boxes that could be opened and closed. The guild coat of arms served as a decorative motif.

As the main purpose of the guild summoning tablets was to convey an order or an invitation to attend a meeting at a given time, some of them were very ingeniously provided with a dial and an adjustable copper pointer to indicate when the meeting, funeral, mass or procession would take place. Tablets such as this were for the most part to be found in the Transdanubian region, Veszprém for example, where tablets with this attachment were owned by the tanners in 1800 (Plate 26); the fullers in 1836; also the potters; this device is also found on a Rococo boot-makers' tablet (Plate 30) now in the Hungarian National Museum. The tablets of the Keszthely potters and the Várpalota fullers exactly resemble a round-faced alarm clock. This type of summoning tablet represents a transition between the "announcing tablets" and the tablets with written messages attached, for the adjustable dial informed members of the time of the meeting in a visible form, though still not in writing.

In some places special tablets were used for summoning the members of the guild to a funeral. These invariably depicted a human skull and in many cases two crossed bones as well. One such funeral summoning tablet which has survived is that of the Késmárk boot-makers' (1733, Ill. 55) which must have been reserved specially for funerals, since another summoning tablet bearing the arms of the guild (Ills. 56–57), used on other occasions, has also survived. The tablet of the Jolsva comb-makers' guild shows a death's-head on the one side, while the other is decorated with the guild emblem, a design based on a comb motif (Plate 14). Obviously they used the side with

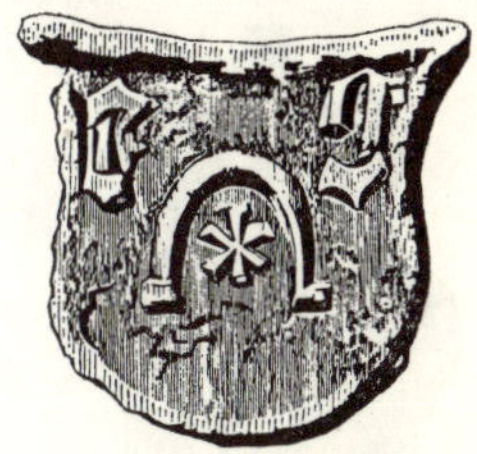

13. The badge of the Nagyszeben carpenters' guild (1504). Brukenthal Museum, Nagyszeben
14. Summoning tablet of a smiths' guild (15th century). Hungarian National Museum, Budapest

the death's-head for funerals. The tablet of the Nagyszeben smiths and gun-makers (1681) is similar in that one side shows a sand-glass symbolizing the transience of life, as well as a skull, while usual symbols of the craft appear on the other side (Ill. 27).

The Style and Art of Summoning Tablets

The shape and decorative motifs of the summoning tablets of the guilds closely followed the major European trends in style: from the late Gothic and Renaissance shield forms, through a series of Late Renaissance and Baroque scroll-decorated cartouches, to the Rococo, Louis XVI, Empire and Classicist pieces, they all show the characteristics lines and decorative elements of the style of their respective periods. The standard of workmanship varies very much, depending on the period and place of origin and the skill of the maker. Some of them are veritable masterpieces, but there are quite primitive pieces too. In the manner of representation and the choice of ornamental motifs they are mostly related to folk art, but in spite of their somewhat provincial appearance, and a charming naiveté, they also reveal a fascinating, if delayed, blend of the prevailing trend of the given period.

The earliest summoning tablet to have been dated with certainty is now in the Nagyszeben Brukenthal Museum. It belonged to the carpenters' guild and is a Late Gothic disc shield carved of hard wood in a somewhat oblique shape, ending in two foils at the base. The numbers scattered between the very finely carved carpenter's tools arranged in a heraldic pattern were interpreted by one scholar as an indication of the year 1450,

15. Summoning badge of the Lőcse coopers' guild (1599). Szepesség Museum
16. Summoning tablet of the Lőcse bakers' guild (1614). Szepesség Museum
17. Summoning badge of the Eperjes knifemakers' guild (1642). East-Slovak Museum, Kassa
18. Summoning badge of the Eperjes locksmiths' guild (1604). Sáros Museum, Bártfa
19–20. Summoning tablet of the Pozsony goldsmiths' guild (17th century). Municipal Museum, Pozsony

but they are "strung on a cord" and should read 1504. The latter figure is corroborated by the shield shape of the tablet (Ill. 13), a shape characteristic of the years around 1500. (The date shown on a guild summoning tablet generally indicates the year in which it was made, but in some cases it refers to the foundation year of the guild. The date can be ascertained by reference to stylistic features of the tablet—as in the case of the one mentioned above.) A second Late Gothic tablet, shield-shaped but symmetrical, is now in the Hungarian National Museum. Unfortunately it bears no date at all, but the minuscule script carved on the obverse indicates that it was made at the end of the fifteenth century. In the centre of the shield, from which the paint is now much worn away, a horse-shoe shaped carved pattern can be traced showing six horse-shoe nails arranged in a star shape at the centre. The other side of the shield is perfectly plain. The size (16×14 cm), the design of the arms on the face and the bored hole above the horse-shoe (Ill. 14), make it seem likely that this was the summoning tablet of a smiths' guild.

The Renaissance summoning tablet of the sixteenth and seventeenth centuries can be classified in two basic groups: the simple Renaissance disc shield and the oval "Rollwerk" cartouche with a scroll border.

The earliest piece among the Renaissance disc shields, and at the same time the most artistic of those which have survived in Hungary, is the ornamented silver summoning badge of the Brassó silversmiths' guild dating from 1556. It is a small masterpiece that has already been described more than once in the literature on goldsmith work

(Plate 3). The fact that it is small and that there is a representation of a workshop scene in relief on the obverse indicates a close relationship with similar ornamental badges of Netherlandish guilds. (See the badge of the Nijmegen guild of sailors. Rijksmuseum, Amsterdam, Ill. 7).

The badge of the Lőcse coopers' guild (Ill. 15), is also sixteenth-century, though it is a much simpler piece. It is a shield of sheet-iron, perfectly shaped in the Renaissance style, a pierced design, a loop and the usual ring. The spiral curls on the two sides of the shield represent already a transition towards the scroll-ornamented cartouches. The pierced design includes the date 1599 and some coopers' tools.

The Lőcse bakers had a similar Renaissance-style sheet-iron armorial disc shield with a fine open-work design including the date 1614 above a regular—still almost Gothic—pretzel outlined with a sensitive feeling for heraldic design (Ill. 16). The Eperjes knifemakers' Renaissance open-work cooper shield bears the date 1642 and is similar in type. In the pattern engraved in the rounded shoulders of the shield the curling lines of the cartouche (Ill. 17) are already discernible. Finally, we may include in the same group the brass tablet of the Eperjes locksmiths dating from 1604 (Ill. 18), which ingeniously combines the outlines of the seventeenth-century "basket-type" lock and the Renaissance armorial disc shield, with a keyhole in the centre and a semicircular loop above.

The simple Renaissance style of armorial disc shield, concave on both sides, was also made in western Hungary, as for example the painted wooden tablet of the Kőszeg button-braiders dating from 1650 (Plate 2). The fine Damascus brocade pattern on the

21. Summoning tablet of the Kassa button-braiders' guild (1669). East-Slovak Museum, Kassa
22. Summoning tablet of the Segesvár comb-makers' guild (1696). Museum of History, Segesvár

background behind the heraldic insignia and the general style of the painting are reminiscent of the sixteenth-century painted armorial shields seen on the letters patent of Hungarian noblemen. A similar finely painted shield-shaped summoning tablet dating from the seventeenth century and in the Renaissance style (Ills. 19–20), once the property of the Pozsony goldsmiths' guild, is now in the Municipal Museum of the town.

The same type of Renaissance-style heraldic shield appeared also in other places; some later examples, however, incorporate a Baroque border. The finest examples are the almost identical guild tablets of the button-braiders of Kassa (1669–1772, Ill. 21), Sárospatak (1710, Plate 1), and Kisszeben.

The simple Renaissance shield survived later than elsewhere in Transylvania, where the Renaissance style persisted strongly and even became popularized. The emblazoners working for the Transylvanian princes long retained the characteristic shield of the Renaissance period, although in time it became strongly provincialized and even distorted. It is natural, therefore, that similar Transylvanian armorial summoning tablets exist dating from various years during the seventeenth and eighteenth centuries, as for example that of the Segesvár comb-makers dating from 1696 (Ill. 22), the Segesvár toolsmiths' tablet with the date 1777 (Ill. 23), and the Nagyszeben button-braiders' tablet from 1709 (Ill. 24).

The carefully carved fine walnut tablet of the Nagyszeben goldsmiths deserves special mention. The cartouche-like shield in which there is almost a hint of the Baroque

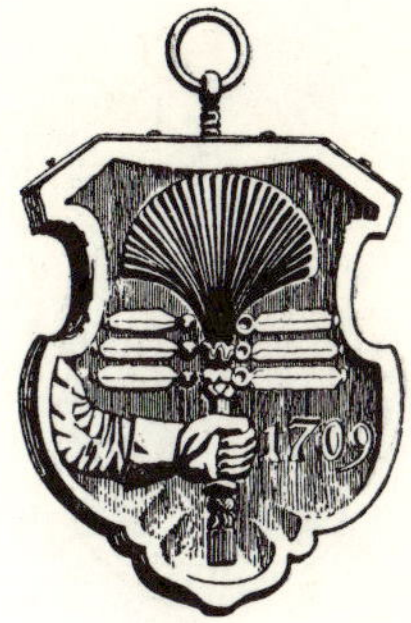

23. Summoning tablet of the Segesvár toolsmiths' guild (1777). Museum of History, Segesvár
24. Summoning tablet of the Nagyszeben button-braiders' guild (1709). Brukenthal Museum, Nagyszeben

indicates a late seventeenth-century origin; however, the angel's head and fruit seen in the decorations, motifs highly characteristic of the Renaissance, show beyond doubt that this is an important and splendid example of Transylvanian workmanship of the Late Renaissance (Ill. 25).

The other type of Renaissance summoning tablet is the oval cartouche with "Rollwerk" or scroll-ornamented border in which the motifs also show a harmonious blending of Renaissance and both the Early and Late Baroque of the seventeenth and eighteenth centuries.

The first known example of this type is the silver mounted tablet of the Szepsi smiths and gunsmiths from 1585 (Plate 4); this is decorated with a border of leaves, ribbons

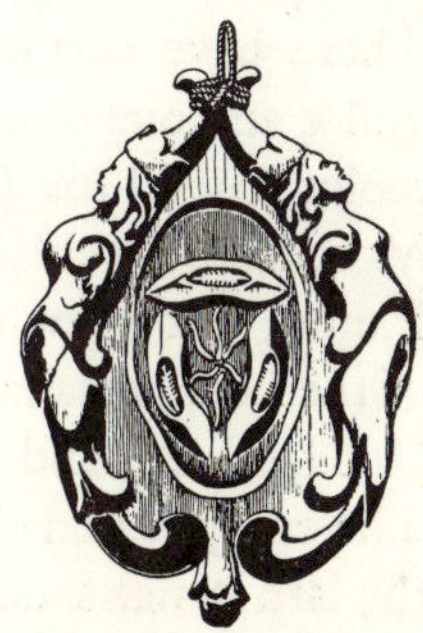

25. Summoning tablet of the Nagyszeben goldsmiths' guild (17th century). Brukenthal Museum, Nagyszeben
26. Summoning tablet of the Rozsnyó weavers' guild (1660). Mining Museum, Rozsnyó

27. Summoning tablet of the Nagyszeben locksmiths and gunsmiths' guild (1681). Museum of History, Kolozsvár
28. Summoning tablet of the Segesvár millers' guild (1648). Historical Museum, Segesvár
29. Summoning tablet of the Nagyszeben hat-makers' guild (18th century). Brukenthal Museum, Nagyszeben
30. Summoning tablet of the Eperjes button-braiders' guild (1663). Slovak National Museum, Pozsony
31–32. Summoning tablet of the Dés boot-makers' guild (1625). Museum of History, Kolozsvár

and cornucopia; other versions of the same design occur on many guild tablets from Upper Hungary and Transylvania. Two of the finest examples are those of the Rozsnyó weavers (1660); on one of these (Ill. 26) we find on either side the hollowed-out figures of two mermaids. Other tablets of this group are those of the Rozsnyó button-braiders from 1653 (Plates 5a–b), the butchers—with the date 1689, also probably from Upper Hungary (Plates 5c–d)—the Ratkó tanners (Plate 42b) and the somewhat later tablet of the Jolsva weavers (1756, Plate 6). Other similar tablets were once owned by the Nagyszeben locksmiths and gunsmiths (1681, Ill. 27), the Segesvár millers (1648, Ill. 28), the Segesvár boot-makers (1691), the Nagyszeben hat-makers (eighteenth century; Ill. 29), and other guilds.

Oval-shaped cartouches, distinctly Baroque in character, though the carving is simple, even primitive, can be found in the Transdanubian region and the Hungarian Plain. There have survived two characteristic examples from Csorna—that of the tailors' guild, and one of a mixed guild dating from 1673 (Plate 7); also the Jászberény tailors' tablet from 1769 (Plate 8).

Most of these shield-shaped painted cartouches were oval, with richly carved wooden frames, but a few made of finely embossed copper are also known, for instance those of the boot-makers' guild of Igló (1658, Plate 9), the button-braiders' guild in Eperjes (1663, Ill. 30) and the bakers' guild in Lőcse (1782).

The complicated shape of a shield with various concaves and convexes deriving from the late Renaissance, already in the style of the Baroque is most decorative. This shape

occurs mainly among tablets from the eighteenth century. They are usually painted, having a carved frame or carving in relief, used chiefly in the northern part of Transdanubia. Surviving examples include the shields of the Devecser boot-makers (1670, Plate 10a), tailors (1715, Plates 11a–b), cartwrights and coopers (1774, Plates 11c–d); also those of the Tósokberénd weavers (1791, Plate 10b) and the boot-makers of Győr (1704) and Székesfehérvár (Plates 12a–b).

There was also a Transylvanian version of the same type, though possibly of somewhat earlier: a multifoiled painted disc shield which, though Renaissance in outline retains more accurately the basic lines of the original shield shape. The finest examples of this type are the tablets of the Dés boot-makers (1625, Ills. 31–32), butchers (1710, Ills. 33–34) and potters (1757, Ill. 35); also that of a Transylvanian tailors' guild (1636, Plate 13). The tablets of the Vajdahunyad potters (Ill. 36) and the Segesvár furriers (1746, Ill. 37) also bear some relationship to this type.

These tablets in which there is a blending of Late Renaissance and Baroque were followed, without any sharp transition by generally asymmetric, elongated C or S-shaped tablets in the Rococo style, marking a gradual departure from the original, almost obligatory shield shape. The finest and most characteristic Rococo tablets come from the Szekszárd boot-makers (1776, see Ill. on jacket), the Fogaras hat-makers (1774), joiners and masons (eighteenth century, Ill. 38), the Jolsva comb-makers (eighteenth century, Plate 14), the Szentgál weavers (1801, Plate 15b) and the Debrecen potters (1804, Plate 16).

33–34. Summoning tablet of the Dés butchers' guild (1710). Museum of History, Kolozsvár

35. Summoning tablet of the Dés potters' guild (1757). Museum of History, Kolozsvár

36. Summoning tablet of the Vajdahunyad potters' guild (18th century). Museum of History, Kolozsvár

37. Summoning tablet of the Segesvár furriers' guild (1746). Museum of History, Segesvár

38. Summoning tablet of the Fogaras joiners' guild (18th century). Brukenthal Museum, Nagyszeben

A strikingly large number of summoning tablets are made in Louis XVI style. This may be due to the fact that this popularized style survived the turn of the century to appear in Hungary in the first decades of the nineteenth century when the guild system was going through a last vigorous revival. Many of these tablets are both beautiful and valuable. The majority are far removed from the shield-shaped tablets; they look more like pictures in nicely carved frames or like small wall-cupboards. It was a style adopted all over the country and beautifully carved pieces adorned with festoons, rosettes, bows, braids and meanders, sometimes in a provincial, popularized form, have survived from as early as the last decade of the eighteenth century. Of these the most characteristic are: the copper-gilt tablet with ribbon decoration of the Kassa bakers dating from 1789 (Ill. 39), the small, elegant "wall-cupboard" (1795), inlaid with a design incorporating a star motif, of the Nagykőrös tailors, the foliated tablet of the Homonna blacksmiths', locksmiths' and bakers' guild (1798, Plate 18), of the Csongrád boot-makers', the fine oval tablet with braided border (1806, Plate 17), of the Gyöngyös harness-makers; also the tablets of the Devecser furriers (1815, Ill. 40), the Tapolcafő weavers (1817, Plate 19), the Nagymihály furriers (1825, Ills. 41–42); and additionally, the copper tablets of the Kolozsvár locksmiths and gunsmiths, all from 1820 (Ills. 43–44) and the most recent example, a copper summoning tablet which belonged to the Strázsa furriers and was made in 1839 (Ill. 77).

The relics of this period include a series of Empire-style summoning tablets. They are, for the most part, in the original shield shape, but naturally with two foils surmounting

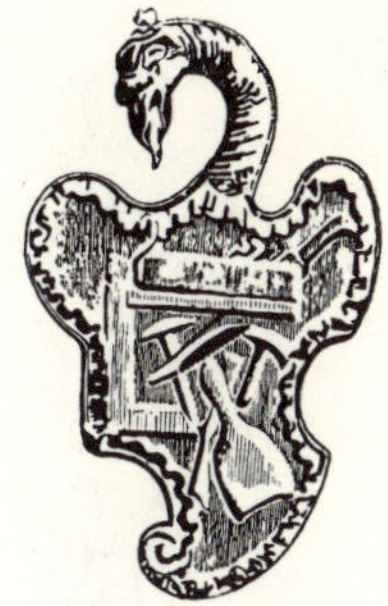

the body of the shield which narrows sharply to end in a pointed base. Metal was much favoured at that time and these typically Empire-style shields were made almost exclusively of brass and were shaped rather like the brass key-plates mounted on contemporary furniture. In many towns the guilds would commission a series of new summoning tablets. Bearing in mind their fundamentally changed function, the shields were now fitted with a letter box on the reverse side, the opening being inscribed with the name of the guild, most of them also bearing a list of the leading members and the year of origin. A number of Empire-style summoning tablets made as described above, have survived from Kassa (Ills. 45–48) and Miskolc (Plates 20–21).
Here and there summoning tablets were also made of wood in popular versions of the Empire style and bearing characteristic symbols of individual crafts. The shield-shaped

39. Summoning tablet of the Kassa bakers' guild (1789). Slovak Museum, Kassa
40. Summoning tablet of the Devecser furriers' guild (1815). Ethnographical Museum, Budapest

tablet in Empire style of the Szentes tailors' guild, with inlaid bone decoration and a centrally placed inscribed copper plate (Plate 23), is an example of this style.

Lastly, there are examples of Neo-Classic architectural solutions, as in the very late tablet decorated with pillars and tympanum (1864, Plate 22) of the Abaújszántó carpenters' and masons' guild.

In addition to the shield-shaped summoning tablets and the types deriving from them, we must mention the tablets which, although still reminiscent of the original shield shape, now begin to assume the outlines of certain folk motifs or popular objects and draw on the rich elements of Hungarian folk art for their ornamentation. The principal group of these would include tablets shaped like a stylized heart or tulip and those reminiscent of chair backs or mirror-frames with folk carvings. Such popular forms and motifs appeared chiefly among the more "rustic" guilds whose products satisfied the simple needs of the rural masses, for instance the guilds of potters, weavers and boot-makers. One of the earliest and finest specimens of this type of tablet belonged to the Pápa potters. It is a heart-shaped lead glazed earthenware summoning badge (1714) with coloured floral decoration possibly still showing Haban influence (Plate 25). Other examples are the flower-decorated boards of the Lőcse potters (1800, Ill. 50) and the Miskolc potters (1854); also the heart-shaped tablets of the Kézdivásárhely joiners (1809) and shoe-makers (1859, Ill. 49); the Andocs weavers (1763) and the Sümeg weavers (1828, Ills. 63–64); the tulip-shaped tablet of the Kézdivásárhely boot-makers (Ill. 51); the tablets of the Veszprém tanners (1800, Plate 26) and the Hód-

41–42. Summoning tablet of the Nagymihály furriers' guild (1825). After Béla Dragoner's study (op. cit. 1879)
43–44. Summoning tablet of the Kolozsvár locksmiths' and gunsmiths' guild (1820). Museum of History, Kolozsvár
45–46. Summoning tablet of the Kassa comb-makers' guild (1833). East-Slovak Museum, Kassa

mezővásárhely boot-makers (1754, Plate 27); and the "letter box" of the Veszprém carpenters with rich, popular carving reminiscent of the so-called *tükrös* (mirror-case, Plate 24).

The announcement tablets constitute another large and quite distinct group of summoning tablets, for they did not develop from the shield and were never made in the shape of a shield. They are rectangular panels with a handle, and constitute in a narrower sense the sign-tablet of the guild. The handle is generally at the bottom, so that the tablet can easily be held aloft to show the "announcement" or the badge itself; but on some of them the handle projects from the upper border. Such tablets are in fact coats of arms, since they generally represent the characteristic emblem of the guild;

47. Summoning tablet of the Kassa tanners' guild (1826). East-Slovak Museum, Kassa
48. Summoning tablet of the Kassa carpenters' and millers' guild (1837). East-Slovak Museum, Kassa

but they also have a certain affinity with the ornamental rods, especially the *ferules*, and may therefore be regarded as a version of the latter—a specifically Hungarian development. These tablets constitute a special combination of the two symbols of authority: the sceptre and the coat of arms.

The earliest surviving example was made as early as the middle of the seventeenth century. The three-foiled ending of the handle and profiled or undulating border ornamentation reflects a Late Gothic and Early Renaissance influence. The wooden tablet of the Kolozsvár joiners with the date 1656 and a representation of a carved Gothic table and a plane (Ill. 52), is also in this category. There is in the Museum of Applied Arts a tablet of the "Hungarian" *passementerie*-makers (1651) with a handle ending in three foils: an unusual feature of this tablet is that the two panel paintings can be taken out of their frames and reversed. On the outer sides there is the traditional arms of the guild—a hand holding a plume and the buttons and lace frogs produced by members of the guild; on the sides are Baroque-style sacred images in oil: Christ on the Cross and the Archangel St. Michael (Plate 28). Very similar tablets were used by the "Hungarian" smiths, and also by the Győr craftsmen, who made shields, bows and spears: on one side of the tablet various arms are shown, on the other the image of St. George the dragon-slayer.

From Transylvania comes the Kolozsvár cartwrights' wooden tablet with the handle carved in Louis XVI style (1827, Ill. 53); but simpler forms of the guild sign with a handle occur also in the Transdanubian region, as for example the Csákvár boot-

49. Summoning tablet of the Kézdivásárhely boot-makers' guild (1859). Gábor Áron Museum, Kézdivásárhely

50. Summoning badge of the Lőcse potters' guild (1800). Szepesség Museum, Lőcse

51. Summoning tablet of the Kézdivásárhely boot-makers (19th century). Gábor Áron Museum, Kézdivásárhely

52. Summoning tablet of the Kolozsvár joiners' guild (1656). Museum of History, Kolozsvár

53. Summoning tablet of the Kolozsvár coopers' guild (1827). Museum of History, Kolozsvár

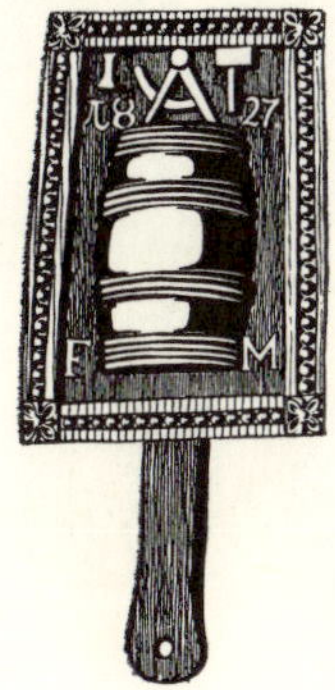

makers' circulating tablet dating from 1760 (Ill. 54) and the Nemeskér boot-makers' tablet.

Summoning and announcing tablets with a handle are most typical in the north-eastern part of the country. The guild tablets from Debrecen, Szatmárnémeti and Munkács are almost exclusively of this type. Some of the tablets of the Munkács and Debrecen guilds, as for example that of the soap-makers (1791, Plate 29), are still of wood, but most of the almost uniform series of tablets produced during the hundred years from around 1750 to 1850 are of copper. They are provided with small hinged frames into which notices could be inserted and read immediately the tablet was held out. In many cases the undulating outlines of this type constitute a reversion to the old shield form, and may therefore be regarded as shields or guilds arms with handles attached.

Heraldry and Iconography

Now having discussed the summoning tablets of old Hungarian guilds, noting their development from the point of view of style and form, especially the basic shield form, we must consider their significance as heraldic devices.

These tablets, generally shield-shaped, or in a form related to the shield, are the most characteristic relics of guild-heraldry and constitute actual tangible objects of the guilds. They differ from most objects in that their original function precludes their

54. Summoning tablet of the Csákvár boot-makers' guild (1760). István Király Museum, Székesfehérvár
55. Funeral summoning tablet of the Késmárk boot-makers' guild (1733). East-Slovak Museum, Kassa
56–57. Summoning tablet of the Késmárk boot-makers' guild (1733). East-Slovak Museum, Kassa
58. Summoning tablet of the Kézdivásárhely butchers' guild (19th century). Gábor Áron Museum, Kézdivásárhely

development from the shields used for self-defence; as miniature shields provided with easily recognizable symbols of authority they merit a place in heraldry somewhere halfway between the "live" or "true" coat of arms used in battle or at tournaments and the summoning seals or other escutcheoned seals found on official documents.
Most summoning tablets conform to the traditional rules of heraldry. Those made of wood generally bore a design in oil, thus meeting the basic requirement that a coat of arms should be coloured. The heraldic motifs on the tablets were usually selected from the most characteristic tools or products of a particular craft. Consequently, the summoning tablets belong, almost without exception, to what are known as canting coats of arms in which there is a clear allusion to a particular craft.
Christian symbolism of the Middle Ages and the Christian manner of representing saints and biblical scenes were widely adopted by the guilds and also influenced the craftsmen who made summoning tablets; it was natural to develop a type of canting arms for many of the saints were associated with particular crafts in which the traditional attributes had their origin.
Decorative heraldic arrangements of tools and craft products are to be found on some tablets dating from the sixteenth, seventeenth and eighteenth centuries—sometimes even on those made in the nineteenth century. Frequently the two most characteristic tools of the craft are shown placed one over the other, e.g. two keys (for the smiths), two pistols (for the gunsmiths), two choppers (for the butchers), two hatchets (for

the carpenters), two stockings (for the hosiers), two wool-bows (for the fullers). Or we find them in a triple arrangement, as for example three shuttles arranged in a triangle (symbolizing the weavers), or a vertically placed fork underneath two crossed knives (symbolizing the knife-makers). There are, however, tablets on which a single tool or product gives a perfect characteristic heraldic bearing, as for example an open pair of tailor's or cropper's scissors, a pretzel, a mill-stone, a single triangular or round hat or a hide looking like a shield. Some bearings on which the design incorporates several tools or products are splendid examples of heraldic emblems, but the representation of too many objects tended to defeat the purpose of the tablet: to communicate by means of symbols that could be interpreted on sight.

The tools and products were often placed between the claws of heraldic beasts, those most frequently represented being two rampant lions but on the bearing of the tanners who used cordovan leather there are two goats (Plate 21). The lion was the favourite heraldic beast in the coats of arms of the Hungarian aristocracy—a decorative element symbolizing nobility, as did another popular motif, the five-pointed crown. Contrary to the practice among members of other Western European guilds, it was customary in the Hungarian guilds to include the epithet "noble", rather than "respected", when addressing members, a custom justified by the fact that most members of the Hungarian guilds came from the lesser nobility, which was not the case in Western Europe generally. This can be explained by the social development peculiar to Hungary, as

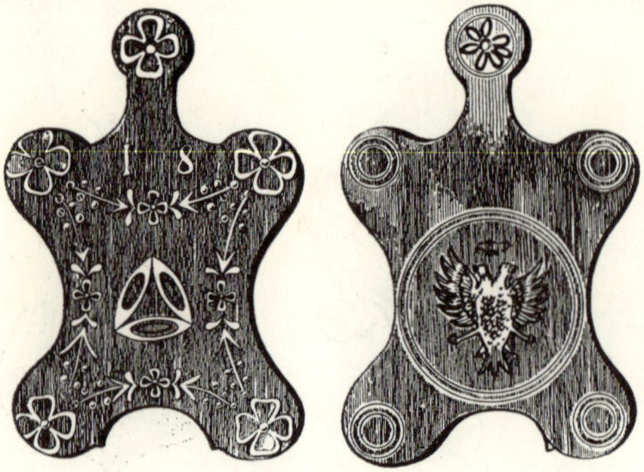

59–60. Summoning tablet of the Nagyatád weavers' guild (1839). Balaton Museum, Keszthely. (Lost)

a result of which the ratio of noblemen to all other classes was the highest in Europe. This disproportionate ratio was due to the fact that the Hungarian nobility counted in its ranks a large number of impoverished squirelings or "petty nobles", all of whom at one time enjoyed equal rights. This development may account to some extent for the relatively rich heraldic material of the Hungarian guilds, including the large number of summoning tablets which have survived, whereas we know of comparatively few armorial bearings of the Hungarian nobility.

Vivid naturalistic representation is characteristic of the heraldic devices of the Hungarian nobility and such scenes are also to be found on many summoning tablets. For instance, the bent arm with a plume which can be seen on the tablet of the button-braiders' guild is a close kin to motifs found on the seventeenth-century patents of Hungarian noblemen which incorporate a bent right arm and hand, the hand gripping a curved sabre (Plates 2 and 5b). Complete scenes, as for example a butcher slaughtering an ox, a tanner cutting leather, a furrier working at his bench, a goldsmith hammering on an anvil, are also frequently found on these tablets.

At first the design of these figural bearings, whether painted or carved, covered the entire tablet, which was in the shape of a shield. Later the tablet was no longer looked upon as a shield, and was indeed not even made in the shape of a shield; it became an object that could be decorated with the bearings of the guild. These tablets were decorated with the accessory elements, the supporters, the crowns to indicate rank and other motifs of the declining art of heraldry, so departing further and further from the world of allusive heraldry.

61–62. Summoning tablet of the Zágráb buttonbraiders' guild (1808).
Croatian History Museum, Zágráb

On some tablets the bearings of the town or country were shown in addition to those of the guild. The double-eagle also occurred in a number of devices, most often in those of the weavers' guilds, as for example in Rozsnyó (seventeenth century), Andocs (1767), Nagyatád (1839, Ills. 59–60) and a few in Zágráb; it figures also on the board of the Lőcse button-makers (1828). The representation of the double-eagle generally indicated the possession of a patent granted by a king or emperor and the small shield on the eagle often contained the royal Habsburg monogram. Until the so-called Bach period (1850s) the motif of the double-eagle was neither unusual nor hateful to the Hungarian people; it appeared even in the weavers' popular patterns and on stove tiles. The arms of the Hungarian State and the Hungarian royal crown also appeared on summoning tablets in many places and in many different versions. There is, for instance, a tablet from the Kassa tailors' guild (1871) decorated only with the Hungarian arms with the crown. The Hungarian royal crown surmounts the shield-shaped summoning tablets of the Kézdivásárhely butchers and weavers (Ill. 58), but the most interesting heraldic solution is a combination of the arms of the Hungarian State and the arms of the guild. A most characteristic example is the tablet of the Vác furriers (1719) on which the four silver fesses in the right field of the Hungarian arms with the apostolic cross and the crown have been replaced by the decorative fur motif (Plate 36) used in the bearings of the craft all over Europe.

The summoning tablet of the Zágráb button-braiders from 1808 shows not only the combined arms of Croatia, Slavonia and Dalmatia but also the arms of the city of Zágráb (Ills. 61–62), while on the tablet of the Jászberény tailors (1769) we find the

63–64. Summoning tablet of the Sümeg weavers' guild (1828). Balaton Museum, Keszthely. (Lost)
65. Summoning tablet of the Zágráb grand guild (of goldsmiths, locksmiths, sword-cutlers, blacksmiths, saddlers, furriers, harness-makers and halberd-makers). (1632–1665). Municipal Museum, Zágráb
66. Summoning tablet of the Lőcse bakers' guild (1782). East-Slovak Museum, Kassa

heraldic motifs of that town—a bent right arm with the apostolic cross and below it the ancient heraldic device of the Jászkun captains, the famous bugle believed to have been in the possession of the tenth-century hero, the Hungarian leader, Lehel (Plate 8). The summoning tablet of the Dobsina miners (1683) corresponds exactly to the town arms.

Representations of the Christian saints are usually in a popularized Baroque style. On the tablet of the Székesfehérvár fullers the mounted figure of St. Martin of Pannonia, known also as St. Martin of Tours, is seen cutting a piece from his cloak to give to a shivering beggar (Plate 37). On the Légrád boatmen's tablet a Noah's Ark has been painted, also the figure of St. Nicholas, the patron saint of sailors; and the Pozsony goldsmiths embellished theirs with the seated figure of St. Eligius wearing a mitre (Ills. 19–20), for the saint too was once a goldsmith. The Sümeg weavers decorated their tablet with a picture of Veronica and the well-known *sudarium* showing the face of Christ (Ills. 63–64). The boot-makers, who pursued a typically Hungarian craft, chose for their tablets Hungarian patron saints, those of Szekszárd showing the Prince, St. Emeric, and those of Székesfehérvár the King, St. Stephen (Plate 12). The Szombathely harness-makers represented St. Paul armed with a sword and holding a book; while the gunsmiths chose to represent St. George, the dragon-slayer, and the button-braiders selected the Archangel St. Michael (Plate 28).

Craft Techniques, Tools and Products

To study the craft techniques illustrated by the summoning tablets we would do well to begin by examining first those showing the masters at work, and then the emblems in which tools and products are depicted.

Of the tablets on which some aspect of a particular craft is illustrated the finest and most interesting is that of the Brassó goldsmiths mentioned earlier. On both sides of the tablet there is a picture of a goldsmith at work in a workshop of the period, the whole scene elaborated with meticulous care (Plate 3). There is also the very interesting copper summoning tablet of the Zágráb Chaptertown's district "grand guild" both sides of which are decorated with beautiful foils and festoons of fruit forming a Baroque shield-like frame within which the field is divided by columns into four vaulted sections in each of which a master is seen at work with his most important tools and products arranged around him. The front illustrates the saddlers', furriers', harness-makers' and spear-makers' crafts, while on the back the work of the goldsmiths, locksmiths and sword-cutlers is shown. It was traditional for the masters of these crafts—in which metal and leather were used for the production of weapons—to unite in one single guild, a tradition handed down from the beginning of the Middle Ages (Ill. 65).

The butchers of Debrecen (1843, Plate 38) and Rohonc (1850) had tablets similarly

67. Summoning tablet of the Rimaszombat butchers' guild (1803). Hungarian National Museum, Budapest. (Lost)
68. Summoning tablet of the Kassa soap-makers' guild (1784). East-Slovak Museum, Kassa

decorated with pictures—in this case showing dogs bringing down an ox and holding it by the ears.

Another vivid representation of a craftsman at work may be seen in the copper emblem dating from the beginning of the nineteenth century showing a tanner about to cut up a hide made of morocco or cordovan leather (Plate 39).

Other crafts were similarly described in pictures, as for instance the furrier working at his bench (Vác, 1719, Plate 36); the harness-maker also busy at his work-bench (Debrecen); a turner of wooden wine-decanters at his lathe (Debrecen, 1828); the soap-maker wearing an apron, with rolled-up shirt-sleeves and a measuring ladle in his hand (Debrecen, 1791, Plate 29); a young weaver holding a ball of thread (Tapolcafő, 1817, Plate 19); and a rope-maker at work (Miskolc, 1826). The tablet of the Buda rope-makers, which dates from 1776 (Plate 40), represents the arrival of a journeyman.

Practically all the characteristic tools and products of the craft industries have been represented on the summoning tablets of the guilds.

Now let us consider the crafts one by one, beginning with the *food industry*.

The *bakers'* emblem shows the pretzel (Lőcse, 1614, Ill. 16), but we also find the crescent-shaped roll, the so-called "imperial roll" and other products (Lőcse, 1782, Ill. 66; Kassa, 1789, 1842, Ill. 39; Szeged, 1832, Plate 41a).

The well-known tablet of the *butchers* shows the head of an ox above two cleavers or pole axes (Rimaszombat, 1803, Ill. 67; Kézdivásárhely, 1870; Kassa, 1836); sometimes

69. Summoning tablet of the Rózsahegy millers' guild (1835). Liptó Museum, Rózsahegy
70. Tablet of the Székelyudvarhely sole-leather tanners' guild (1584/1830). Private collection (?), Székelyudvarhely

these symbols are surrounded by knives and a whittle (see tablet of an unknown butchers' guild from 1689, Plate 5c; also the tablet from Dés, 1710, Ills. 33–34).

As both soap and tallow candles were made from suet we find that the emblem of the Kassa *soap-makers* dating from the year 1784 shows a block of soap and a bundle of candles (Ill. 68).

The tablet of the *millers* represents a mill-wheel—that ancient means of harnessing the power of water—as on the Segesvár millers' tablet (1648, Ill. 28). In the emblem of the Veszprém millers (1797, Plate 42a), the wheel is surmounted by a pair of calipers. One may frequently find other carpenters' tools in the millers' bearings, as for example in that of the Rózsahegy guild (1835, Ill. 69), indicating that, besides grinding corn, the millers often built their own mills (see millers carving wood on the tablet of the Kassa carpenters' and millers' guild from 1837, Ill. 48).

The *leather and tanning industry* developed from the ancient boot and shoe-makers' craft, which originally united the different phases of leather-dressing and shoe-making. This is reflected in the emblem on the tablet of the Székelyudvarhely shoe-makers. One side of it shows the carved image of a typical tool used in tanning and known as the crutch; it is a crescent-shaped iron for softening and smoothing the leather. The other side bears a picture of shoe-making tools: the hatchet-shaped knife and the awl used during the sewing process (Ills. 72–73).

The tablet of the *tanners*—whose work was confined to dressing the leather—showed

71. Summoning tablet of the Jolsva tanners' guild (1829). East-Slovak Museum, Kassa
72–73. Summoning tablet of the Székelyudvarhely shoemakers' guild. Private collection (?), Székelyudvarhely
74. Summoning tablet of the Székelyudvarhely boot-makers' guild (1635). Private collection (?), Székelyudvarhely
75. Summoning tablet of the Székelyudvarhely harness-makers' guild (1779). Museum, Székelyudvarhely

the tanning vat and two scudding-knives (Székelyudvarhely, 1584, 1830, Ill. 70), or two scudding-knives arranged crosswise over a vertically placed leather carving knife (Szentes, 1823). The tablets of the Kassa (1826) and Jolsva (1829) tanners show a master standing in his tanning vat (Ill. 71). A similar picture is seen on the tablet of the Veszprém tanners (1800, Plate 26). The master tanners in the Transdanubian region were called "white"-tanners. Unlike other tanners who worked with ox and calf hide, they produced fine morocco and cordovan leather from sheep and kid hide. They also followed a different tanning process, using sumac and the droppings of dogs instead of tannic acid. In other parts of the country the tanner producing morocco and cordovan leather from sheep and goat hide was called *cordovan tanner*. The two rampant goats holding the usual tanning tools seen in the tablet of the Miskolc cordovan tanners (1855, Plate 21) refer to this special branch of tanning.

The largest number of summoning tablets have come down to us from the *boot-makers*. This can be readily understood if we consider that the craft had the largest number of guilds in Hungary. Their emblem, adopted nation-wide, was the boot —generally depicted together with the two most characteristic tools of the trade, the sleeker, a copper tool with a knob for smoothing the leather and the leather cutting knife which resembled a hatchet. This type of emblem can be seen on the summoning tablets of the boot-makers of Dés (1625, Ills. 31–32), Székelyudvarhely (1635, Ill. 74), Igló (1658, Plate 9), Jolsva (1829), Devecser (1670, 1844, Plate 10a) and Peremarton (1770, Plate 15a). On some of them there are two boots in different colours (Devecser,

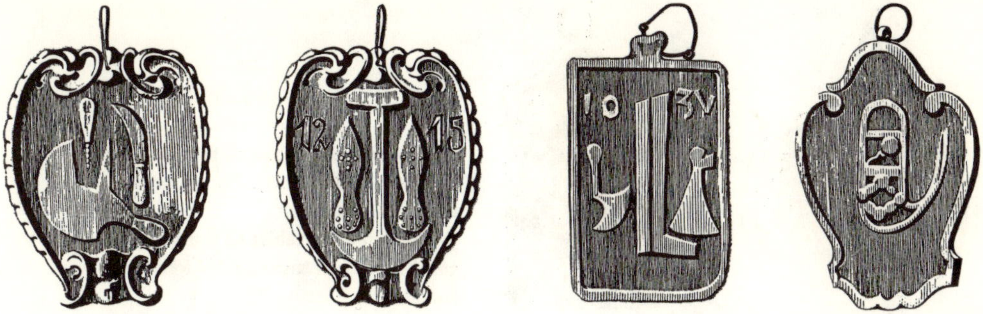

1670; Mór, 1815) or two different hatchet-shaped leather cutting knives, while on the tablet of the Késmárk boot-makers (1733) the device includes a slipper as well as a high-heeled woman's boot (Ills. 56–57). Some of the boots are stitched on their sides and are higher at the front than the back. Some have spurs attached to them (Debrecen, 1808), while others are shown together with a kind of sandal (Dés, 1625; Balassagyarmat, 1719, Plate 43; and Székesfehérvár).

The most characteristic symbols of the *harness-makers*, the bridle and the collar, can be seen on guild tablets from Székelyudvarhely (1779, Ill. 75), Gyöngyös (1806, Plate 17), and Kolozsvár (1820), generally represented bent like the stem of a pipe.

The tablet of the famous Hungarian *saddlers* of Tiszafüred (Ill. 76) shows a complete set of tools for this craft. Looking at the small wooden tablets carved in a popular style and showing the dates 1823 and 1849, it is hard to believe that when Frederick the Great set up the Prussian cavalry he had saddlers brought from Tiszafüred to introduce the Hungarian-type saddles to Prussia.

Another ancient craft associated with the leather industry is that of the *furriers*. Their distinguishing emblem is a piece of fur usually represented in the form of a shield: Segesvár, 1746 (Ill. 37); Devecser, 1814 (Ill. 40); Strázsa, 1839 (Ill. 77). In the emblem of the Vác furriers it was incorporated into the Hungarian national arms (1719, Plate 36) together with the most important tool of the furriers, a bench on which there is a blade resembling a scythe; a furry animal with a long tail, a fox or a marten, can be seen in the lower part of the tablet. The tablet of the furriers of Nagymihály is

76. Summoning tablet of the Tiszafüred saddlers' guild (1823). Ethnographical Museum, Budapest
77. Summoning tablet of the Strázsa furriers' guild (1839). Hungarian National Museum, Budapest

unique since, in addition to the furriers' tools, it shows the figure of a bear standing on its hind legs (Ills. 41–42).

The most important ancient craft connected with the *iron* and *metal industry* is that plied by the *smiths*. The symbols figuring most frequently on their summoning tablets are the horse-shoe and the shoeing tools (the farrier's pliers, hammer, butteris and rasp). They appear on the fifteenth-century tablet of the Segesvár blacksmiths now in the Hungarian National Museum, the seventeenth-century tablet from Nagyrőce (1803, Ill. 78) and a tablet from Kolozsvár bearing the date 1820. The tool-makers form a separate group. This is evident from another tablet also from Segesvár (1777) showing two crossed scythes, a hoe and an axe (Ill. 23).

The *gunsmiths* and *locksmiths* generally combined in one guild. Two keys arranged crosswise and a gun or pistol are the craft symbols found on their guild tablets (Ill. 80). The earliest of these, dating from 1585, belonged to the Szepsi locksmiths and gunsmiths. Besides the symbols already mentioned, it shows a spur, a stirrup and a spontoon (Plate 4). Painted on the tablet of the gunsmiths and locksmiths of Veszprém there is a ribbed-headed war-hammer below two pistols arranged crosswise (1725, Plate 32), while the design on the tablet of the Nagyszeben guild includes a hammer (1681). In the emblem of the Miskolc locksmiths (1718) these same symbols are found within a round, pierced frame (Plate 31).

The *spur-makers* of Pozsony had a guild of their own. Their tablet—provided with a ong handle—shows a pair of spurs and a curb-bit (Ill. 79).

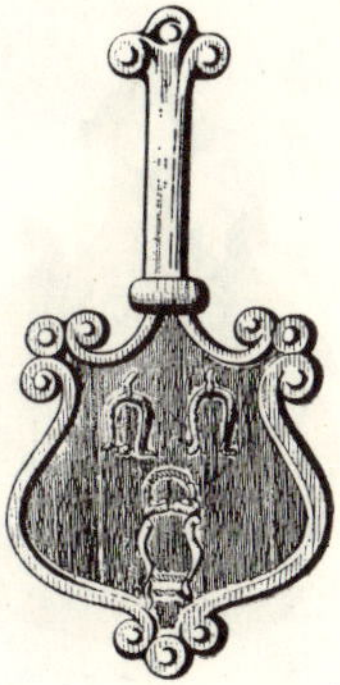

78. Summoning tablet of the Nagyrőce blacksmiths' guild (1803). Slovak National Museum, Pozsony
79. Summoning tablet of the Pozsony spur-makers' guild (17th century). Municipal Museum, Pozsony

The locksmiths of Kolozsvár added two knives to their tablet (1820, Ills. 43–44), but in some places, as for example in Eperjes, the *knife-makers* formed a separate guild. Their open-work copper emblem (1642) represents a foiled crown pierced cross-wise by two knives with a two-pronged fork placed upright between them (Ill. 17).
The emblems of other kindred but highly specialized crafts associated with the iron and metal industry can be seen on the tablet of the so-called united guild of Miskolc (1812). It shows the anvil and tools of the *master braziers* (or *Gürtler*, belt-makers), the chess figure of a knight symbolizing the *turners*, the bow-drill and products of the *needlers*, a figure holding armour representing the *tinsmiths* and, in the lower part of the tablet, one of the most interesting signs, that of the *pewterers* and *braziers*, a design incorporating a gun-barrel, a can, a bell and a quadrangular flask, set between two elephants' trunks from which seven little flags project sideways. Elephant trunks figure in the crest of the ancient coat of arms of Thuringia, and in the pewterers' emblem they symbolize this area, the richest source of tin ore in Europe and cradle of the tinsmiths' craft (Plate 20).
Finally, the beautifully made tablets of the *goldsmiths*' guilds show the finest products of a craft, which is really a branch of the applied arts. For their tablet the Nagyszeben gold and silversmiths chose to represent a gold goblet and a silver spoon (Ill. 25), the Pozsony goldsmiths a ring with a precious stone and one half of the belt for a *mente* (Hungarian short fur-lined dolman-like jacket; Ills. 19–20).
The essential basic materials of the *textile* and *textile-processing industries* were produced

80. Summoning tablet of the gun-makers and locksmiths (1695). Hungarian National Museum, Budapest
81. Summoning tablet of the Nagyszeben wool-weavers' guild (1739). Museum of History, Kolozsvár
82–83. Funeral tablet of the Zsolna croppers' guild (1824). Slovak National Museum, Pozsony
84. Tablet of the Rozsnyó cape-makers' (gubások) guild (1864).Mining Museum, Rozsnyó

by the fullers and the weavers. The *fullers* (wool websters) of Székesfehérvár included in their emblem (Plate 37) a variety of their tools including the highly characteristic *wool-bows*, which can also be seen doubled and placed crosswise in the tablet of the Nagyszeben fullers (1739, Ill. 81). Cropping was a special branch of the clothmakers' craft. The cloth croppers of Zsolna represented a characteristic pair of open cropper shears, reminiscent of sheep shears, on their summoning tablet (1824, Ills. 82–83). The wool industry included the weaving of the peasant-cape known as *guba.* The men plying this craft were known as *gubások.* Engraved on the tablet of the *gubások* of Rozsnyó (1864, Ill. 84) we find a wool breaker, a card and a spinning wheel. Finally, the *hat-makers'* craft was also associated with the textile industry, since felt hats were made of wool. Thus the Rozsnyó hat-makers' tablet shows the wool-bow together with other tools of the craft (1766, Ill. 85). Other hat-makers' guilds preferred to show hats of various shapes: the Nagyszeben guild a three-cornered hat (Ill. 29); the Fogaras guild a broad-brimmed hat; and the Miskolc guild a hat fashionable in 1815 when the tablet was made (Plate 20b).

Very many *weavers'* tablets exist, for after the boot-makers' guilds, the weavers' guilds were more numerous than any other craft. Their tablets were almost always composed of three shuttles arranged in a triangle. This sign was used by the Rozsnyó weavers as early as in the seventeenth century (Ill. 26). It is to be found on the tablets of the weavers of Segesvár (1777), Szentgál (1801, Plate 15b) and other places, sometimes completed with a ball of thread in the middle of the triangle.

A good number of the summoning tablets of the *tailors'* guilds have also survived. Their device, found throughout Europe, was a pair of open scissors. On the earliest of these tablets the ears of the scissors are in the medieval open S-shape. This emblem can be seen on the tablet of a very old guild (1636, Plate 13) which is now in the Hungarian National Museum; also on guild tablets from Fertőszentmiklós (1645, Plate 34) and Bártfa (1703, Ill. 86) and on one tablet of unknown provenance (1723, Plate 44). Later summoning tablets, such as that of the tailors of Devecser (1715, Plates 11a–b), Szomolnok (1759, Plate 45) and Jászberény (1769, Plate 8) show scissors with round closed ears. On these later tablets, in addition to the scissors, we find also the tailors' stiletto and large-headed pins; while that of the Jászberény guild includes a thimble and gooses.

The tailors who made the long, embroidered *szűr* (frieze) mantles, the characteristic feature of Hungarian peasant wear—were called *szűr*-makers. This mantle can be seen on the tablet of the *szűr-tailors* of Miskolc (1869, Plate 46b). A yardstick and a pair of open scissors, the most important tools of the craft, are also incorporated in the design. The book-shaped summoning tablet of the Debrecen *szűr*-makers' guild is very similar (Plate 46a).

Only one tablet (1725) of the *stocking-knitters'* guild is known. This depicts a pair of open scissors, but the chief motifs are a pair of long stockings and a wool shredder (Plate 33).

The traditional bearing of the *rope-makers* shows a flax-comb, two twisting irons ar-

85. Tablet of the Rozsnyó hat-makers' guild (1766). Mining Museum, Rozsnyó
86. Summoning badge of the Bártfa tailors' guild (1703). Sáros Museum, Bártfa

ranged crosswise, and an arrow, all enclosed within a heart-shaped motif. This emblem can be seen on the tablet of the rope-makers of Buda (1776, Plate 40).

The braided cord froggings and buttons for the Hungarian national costume were produced by the *button-braiders.* Button-braiding was one of the most characteristic of Hungarian handicrafts. Even in Vienna there was a Hungarian button-braiders' guild. The device was almost always the same—possibly an indication that an early guild had at some time received letters patent from the king. The emblem shows a bent right arm, a plume in the hand, and on either side various decorative froggings and buttons. It is found on the tablets from Kőszeg (1650, Plate 2), Kassa (1669, 1772), Sárospatak (1710, Plate 1), Nagyszeben (1709, Ill. 24) and Rozsnyó (1653, Plates 5a–b). The last mentioned differs from the others in that the reverse also bears various tools of the craft. On each of the two tablets of the Zágráb button-braiders (1750 and 1808) we find representations of two men in contemporary Hungarian costume richly decorated with button-braiders' products (Ills. 87 and 61–62).

The earliest surviving guild tablets associated with the *timber and building industries* are those of the *coopers.* That of the Lőcse coopers (1599) represents a pair of coopers' compasses, a mallet and some hoop driving tools (Ill. 15). The tablet from Nagyszeben shows various coopers' products and bears the year 1582, although the barrel-shaped tablet itself is probably of later date. The wooden compasses on the tablet of the Kolozsvár coopers' guild are already of the bow-compass type (1827, Ill. 53). A similar instrument is seen on the tablet of the coopers' guild of Rózsahegy (Ill. 88) and the

87. Summoning tablet of the Zágráb button-braiders' guild (1750). Croatian History Museum, Zágráb
88. Summoning tablet of the Rózsahegy coopers' guild (19th century). Liptó Museum, Rózsahegy

wet-coopers' guild of Devecser (1774, Plate 11d). The cooper, wet-cooper and hooper are different names for the same ancient craft of making wooden vessels and barrels.
The reverse of the summoning tablet of the Devecser coopers shows the emblem of another ancient craft associated with the timber industry, that of the *wheelwrights* or cartwrights, who formed a joint guild with the local coopers. The wheelwrights' principal motif was the wheel. It is represented encircled by other implements used in the craft—the hatchet, broad-axe and drawing knife (Plate 11c). The tablet of the Kassa wheelwrights (1703, 1811) is simpler, bearing only a painted wheel and a pair of compasses (Ill. 89). But those of the Nagyszeben (1769, Ill. 90) and Miskolc (1841) cartwrights are all the more elaborate, each one showing an elegant carriage with a hood.
Of the surviving *joiners'* summoning tablets that of the Kolozsvár guilds shows a plane with a table below, the style being still almost Gothic (1656, Ill. 52). Later tablets of this same craft show the plane, the trying-square and the compasses, as for example the Sopron emblem (1842, Plate 48); but chisels and hammers are also often included (see the eighteenth-century tablet of the joiners of Fogaras, Ill. 38).
The *carpenters'* tablets are decorated with a variety of tools used in the craft, as the adze, the broad-axe, the carpenter's axe, the hatchet, the bevel square. The oldest carpenters' tablet known to us is that of the Nagyszeben guild (1504); this shows various types of axe, a saw and an iron chain (Ill. 13). Almost every tool used in the craft from the cramp-iron to the cross-cut saw was commissioned by the Veszprém carpenters to be carved on a tablet which was designed to carry written messages

89. Summoning tablet of the Kassa wheelwrights' guild (1703). East-Slovak Museum, Kassa
90. Summoning tablet of the Nagyszeben cartwrights' guild (1769). Brukenthal Museum, Nagyszeben

(Plate 24). The emblem of the Bártfa carpenters (1738) is of special interest. It is an onion-shaped copper plate intended to represent in silhouette a Baroque helm roof, thus indicating the carpenter's most exacting task, the building of the timber structure for such a roof. The carpenters often combined with the millers in one guild, so that one may find their symbols together with the mill-wheel and the millstone "distaff" as on the tablets of the Csongrád carpenters and millers (see back of jacket), and the Kassa carpenters and millers (1837, Ill. 48).
Another possible combination was for the carpenters to form a guild together with the masons. One finds, for instance, on the Abaújszántó tablet (1864) an emblem which includes masons', brick-burners' and carpenters' tools (Plate 22).
As we have already seen on the tablet from Miskolc, the *turners*' symbol was a chess piece (the knight), but in addition to this they often included in their emblem a compass and a turned skittle-pin.
The *comb-makers* who fashioned their products from horn also showed both their tools and their products on their tablets. On that of the Segesvár comb-makers (1696) a comb was painted at the centre of a motif of red flowers on one side, and a saw on the other (Ill. 22). The tablet of the Kassa comb-makers (1833) shows two lions holding a back-comb with an ornamental border; below this a barber's comb, one half with fine teeth, the other with coarse teeth (Ills. 45–46). There is a similar emblem on the tablet of the Jolsva comb-makers' guild (Plate 14).
Finally we must note the remarkable variety of summoning tablets of the *potters*,

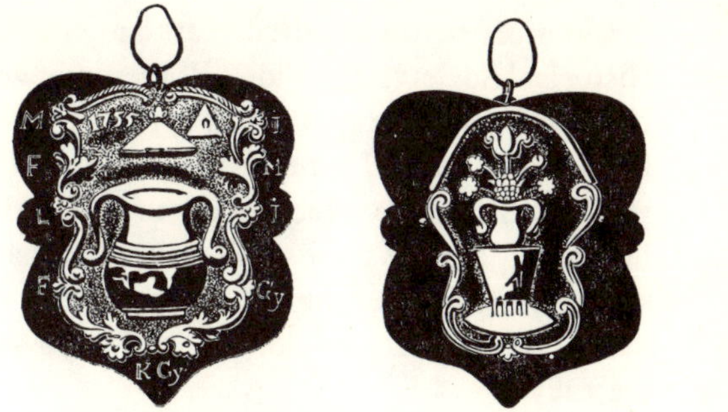

91–92. Tablet of the Rozsnyó potters' guild (1755). Mining Museum, Rozsnyó

whose medium was clay. These are generally decorated with floral patterns—not only because floral ornamentation is characteristic of Hungarian folk art, but also because it was the potters who made simple flower pots: Pápa (1714, Plate 25); Rozsnyó, 1755, (Ills. 91–92); Segesvár, 1766; Lőcse (1800, Ill. 50); Miskolc, 1852. The most important implement of the craft, the wheel, is usually included in the potters' emblems. The Pápa tablet still shows a medieval type of revolving drum, but those from Vajdahunyad and Lőcse depict a more recent type of potter's wheel with axle and two discs; also the inevitable triangular wooden knives used by potters. The two-eared "Italian pitcher", familiar since the Renaissance, has almost become the sole emblem of pottery; nevertheless, other everyday products, for example the long-necked jug and the saucepan with treble feet are also included in the potters' tablets, for example in that of the Dés potters (1757, Ill. 35).

Craftsmen at work, tools and products seen on summoning tablets illustrate a standard of technical accomplishment among craftsmen in Hungary which remained almost constant for four hundred years. They provide us with an authentic picture of the tools and equipment of a few long extinct crafts, and constitute a valuable source for scholars studying the history of costume and other aspects of cultural history.

★

It was more than a hundred years ago, on March 1, 1877, in an address to the Hungarian Historical Society, that Flóris Rómer, pioneer in the fields of Hungarian archaeology and the history of Hungarian art, spoke of the significance of the Hungarian guilds in the history of culture. He referred not only to the literary sources but also to the important relics of the guilds which have survived. He it was who first queried the extent of our heritage. "Do the guilds still possess treasures, guild-chests, seals, jugs, goblets, flags, summoning tablets" he asked, "and if so, from what date, and have they any artistic value? If they are no longer in the possession of the guilds or towns, then where are they?"

It was as a result of this appeal that scholars began to collect, in a systematic and scientific manner, every kind of documentary and physical evidence of the guilds in Hungary. More recently, a computer has been used by research workers engaged in listing surviving records of Hungarian handicraft guilds—but the comprehensive programme envisaged by Rómer is as yet unfulfilled. No definitive publication on the history of the guilds has appeared to date, and there are serious gaps to be filled in our knowledge of individual aspects of the subject. There has been no attempt to compare and analyse on a national scale the guild relics which have survived throughout the country.

This brief survey is intended to answer only a single question raised by Rómer, namely whether the summoning tablets of the Hungarian guilds possessed any artistic, cultural or historic value. We believe that the tablets we have described, selected from around 500 summoning tablets surviving from more than forty different crafts plied in one hundred and twenty Hungarian towns and villages, will give an unequivocally positive reply—however delayed—to the question posed a hundred years ago.

In conclusion I should like to pay tribute to the memory of the late Dr. László Nagy, whose pioneer work in this field inspired me to commence my own research; and secondly to all the directors and staff of the museums and institutes in Hungary and abroad who have assisted me in the preparation of this book by giving me access to the relics in their care and permission to publish this account of them.

References

a. *The Development of the Guild System, its Organization and Surviving Relics*

BÁCSKAI, VERA: *Magyar mezővárosok a XV. században* [Hungarian Market-towns in the Fifteenth Century]. Budapest, 1965.

EPERJESSY, GÉZA: *Mezővárosi és falusi céhek az Alföldön és a Dunántúlon (1686—1848)* [Market-Town and Village Guilds in the Hungarian Plain and the Transdanubian Region. 1686–1848]. Budapest, 1967.

ÉRI, ISTVÁN—NAGY, LAJOS—NAGYBÁKAY, PÉTER: *A magyarországi céhes kézművesipar forrásanyagának katasztere.* I–II. [The Bibliography of Hungarian Craft Guilds. I–II]. Budapest, 1975–1976.

HOUDEK, IVAN: *Cechovnictvo na Slovensku.* Turciansky Sväty Martin, 1943.

LÉDERER, EMMA: "A legrégibb magyar iparososztály kialakulása" [The Development of the Earliest Artisan Class in Hungary]. *Századok*, 1928.

PASCU, STEFAN: *Mestesugurile din Transilvania plna in secolul al XVI.-lea.* Bucureşti, 1954.

ŠPIESZ, ANTON: *Remeslo na Slovensku v obdobi existencie cechov.* Bratislava, 1972.

SZÁDECZKY, LAJOS: *Iparfejlődés és a céhek története Magyarországon* [Industrial Development and the History of Guilds in Hungary]. Budapest, 1913.

SZŰCS, JENŐ: *Városok és kézművesség a XV. századi Magyarországon* [Towns and Handicrafts in Fifteenth-century Hungary]. Budapest, 1955.

b. *The Summoning Tablet—Customs, Development and History*

CSAPLOVICS, JÁNOS: "Mesteremberek czéhbeli régiségeik" [Antiquities of Craft Guilds]. *Tudományos Gyűjtemény.* (1823). VI. p. 48.

GYÖRFFY, ISTVÁN—VISKI, KÁROLY: *A magyarság néprajza. Tárgyi néprajz.* II. 2. kiadás [The Ethnography of the Magyars. Ethnographic Relics]. II. 2nd edition.

HORNYIK, JÁNOS: "Az idézőpecsétről" [The Summoning Seal]. *Magyar Akadémiai Értesítő, Philosophiai, törvény- és történettudományi oszt.* [Bulletin of the Hungarian Academy. Dept. of Philosophy Jurisprudence and Historical Science]. Vol. IV. 1864. pp. 41–53.

JAKUBOVICH, EMIL: "I. Endre király törvénybe idéző ércbilloga" [Metal Summoning Seal of King Andrew I.]. *Turul* (1933). pp. 56–74.

OREND, MISCH: *Siebenbürger Sachsen.* Leipzig, 1937.

RICHTER, M. ISTVÁN: "A céhlegények gyűlése. A németprónai céhek életéből" [The Journeymen's Assembly. From the Story of the Németpróna Guilds]. *Ethnographia* (1920–22, 1923). pp. 101–110.

RICHTER, M. ISTVÁN: "A pénz megtisztelése. Németprónai céhszokás" [The Honouring of Money. A Guild Custom at Németpróna]. *Ethnographia* (1918). pp. 256–271.

RÖSLER, RUDOLF: *Beitrag zur Geschichte des Zunftwesens. Älteres Zunftwesen in Hermannstadt bis zum Jahre 1526.* Hermannstadt, 1912.

SCHULLERUS, ADOLF, D. DR.: *Siebenbürgisch-sächsische Volkskunde im Umriß.* Leipzig, 1926.

SIEBER, SIEGFRIED: "Nachbarschaften, Gilden, Zünfte und ihre Feste." I–II. *Archiv für Kulturgeschichte* Bd. 11 und 12. (1913–14). p. 455; (1914–16), p. 56.

VISKI, KÁROLY: "Bírópecsét. Egy Árpád-kori szokás emléke" [Court Seal. Relic of a Custom from the Age of the Árpáds]. *Népünk és Nyelvünk.* (1930). pp. 98–110.

c. *Summoning Badges of Guilds in Other European Countries*

ANGELOTTI, ANNA MARIA, E.: *Statuto dell'Arte della Lana di Firenze (1317–1319) Fonti I.*, Florence, 1940.

ANKERT, HEINRICH: "Amtszeichen, Ladungszeichen und Aehnliches im nördlichen Theile Böhmens." *Zeitschrift für Österreichische Volkskunde* VII (1901). pp. 105–116.

DE FRANCESCO, GRETE: "Vom Sinn der Handwerkszeichen." CIBA-*Rundschau*, Basel, 1937. Mai. pp. 422–453.

DE VIGNE, FÉLIX: *Recherches historiques sur les costumes civiles et militaires des gildes et des corporations de métiers, leurs drapeaux, leurs armes, leurs blasons*, etc., Gand, 1847.

DE VIGNE, FÉLIX: *Mœurs et usages des corporations de métiers de la Belgique et du Nord de la France pour faire suite aux Recherches historiques sur les costumes civiles et militaires des gildes et des corporations de métiers*, etc., Gand, 1857.

ERPERS ROIJAARDS, F. VAN: *Pronk der gilden.* Amsterdams Historisch Museum, 15 mei tot 6 juli 1964. [Catalogue of Exhibition.]

GRÖBER, KARL: *Alte deutsche Zunftherrlichkeit.* München, 1936.

HÁLOVÁ-JAHODOVÁ, CECILIE: *Vergessene Handwerkskunst.* Prague, 1955.

ISENBERG, HEINRICH: *Altes Brauchtum in Handwerk. Das Gesellenwandern und was damit zusammenhing.* Münster i.W., 1934.

NISSEN, ROBERT: "Silberne Boten- und Spielmannsabzeichen und ihre Träger." *Westfahlen. Hefte für Geschichte und Volkskunde* Bd. 36. (1958). Heft 3. pp. 167–191.

SCHMIDT, LEOPOLD: *Zunftzeichen, Zeugnisse alter Handwerkskunst.* Salzburg, 1973.

SCHUTTER, G. N.—WESTERS, A.: *De Groningse gilden.* Groninger Museum voor Stad en Lande. 21 december 1966 tot en met 22 januari 1967. [Catalogue of exhibition.]

THIKÖTTER, ELISABETH: *Die Zünfte Bremens im Mittelalter.* Bremen, 1930.

d. *Summoning Tablets of Guilds in Hungary*

BIELZ, JULIUS DR.: "Die Zunftaltertümer im Baron Brukenthalischen Museum." *Mitteilungen aus dem Brukenthalischen Museum* VI. Hermannstadt [Nagyszeben] (1936–37). pp. 5–21.

BODÓ, SÁNDOR: "Céhbehívótáblák a miskolci Herman Ottó Múzeumban" [Summoning Tablets of Guilds in the Miskolc Herman Ottó Museum]. *Herman Ottó Múzeum Évkönyve* [Yearbook of the Herman Ottó Museum]. (1968). pp. 171–211.

BODÓ, SÁNDOR: "Két miskolci céhbehívótábla és két névsortábla" [Two Summoning Tablets and Two Ferules with Guild Members' Roll from Miskolc]. *A miskolci Herman Ottó Múzeum Közleményei* 8 (1969). pp. 37–42.

BUNTA, MAGDALENA–IOSUB, VIORICA: "Tabele si semnele de breasla in colectiile muzeeler de Istorie Cluj si Sighişoara" [Guild Tablets and Badges in the Kolozsvár and Segesvár Museum of History]. *Acta Musei Napocensis* IV (1967). pp. 199–214.

DEÁK, FARKAS: "Régészeti kalászok Pozsonyból és vidékéről" [Archaeological Finds from the Pozsony Area]. *Archaeologiai Értesítő* (1877). pp. 259–264.

DIVALD, KORNÉL: "Csongrádi céhemlékek" [Guild Relics from Csongrád]. *Magyar Iparművészet* (1903). pp. 136–138.

DRAGONER, BÉLA: "Zemplén megyében fekvő Nagymihály mezőváros czéhpecsétjei" [Guild Seals of the Market-town Nagymihály in Zemplén County]. *A Felső-Magyarországi Múzeum Egylet harmadik évkönyve* [Third Yearbook of the Museum Association of Upper Hungary]. Kassa, (1879).

INCZE, LÁSZLÓ: "Céhpecsétek és céhbehívótáblák a kézdivásárhelyi múzeum gyűjteményében" [Seals and Summoning Tablets of Guilds in the Kézdivásárhely Museum]. ALUTA, *a Sepsiszentgyörgyi Múzeum Évkönyve* [ALUTA, Yearbook of the Sepsiszentgyörgy Museum], VI–VII (1974–1975). pp. 113–142.

JAKOB, KÁROLY DR.: *Látogatás a főiskola régiségtárában a céhek emlékei között* [A Visit to the Archaeological Department of the College. Guild Relics]. Sárospatak, 1944.

A Kassai Múzeum gyűjteményeinek leíró lajstroma. [Descriptive Catalogue of the Collections of the Kassa Museum]. Kassa, 1903.

KOMÁROMY, JÓZSEF: "A jászberényi céhélet két emléke" [Two Relics of Guild Life in Jászberény]. *A jászberényi Jász Múzeum Évkönyve 1938–1943* [Yearbook of the Jászberény Jász Museum. 1938–1943]. Budapest, (1943). p. 152.

MIHALIK, JÓZSEF: *Vezető a Sárosmegyei Múzeum gyűjteményeiben Bártfán* [Guidebook, Sáros County Museum, Bártfa]. Kassa, 1906. pp. 100–102.

MIHALIK, SÁNDOR: *A Miklós-börtön* [The Miklós Prison]. Kassa, 1942.

NAGY, LÁSZLÓ DR. által a történelmi Magyarország különböző múzeumaiban őrzött céhbehívótáblákról összegyűjtött fényképanyag a veszprémi Bakonyi Múzeumban [Photographic material in the Veszprém Bakony Museum showing guild summoning tablets now in the history museums of Hungary].

NAGYBÁKAY, PÉTER: "Veszprémi és Veszprém megyei céhbehívótáblák" [Guild Summoning Tablets from Veszprém and Veszprém County]. *Veszprém Megyei Múzeumok Közleményei* II (1964). pp. 341–363.

NAGYBÁKAY, PÉTER: "Munkaeszközábrázolások magyarországi céhjelvényeken" [The Representation of Tools on Hungarian Guild Badges]. *Technikatörténeti Szemle* IV (1967). pp. 171–189.

NÄGLER, DOINA: "Tablele de Breaela ale Muzeului Brukenthal" [Guild Summoning Tablets in the Brukenthal Museum]. *Acta Musei Napocensis* IV (1967). pp. 199–214.

NYÁRY, ALBERT BR. DR.: "Iglói csizmadiák és gombkötők" [Boot-makers and Button-makers of Igló]. *Néprajzi Értesítő*, (1905).

NYÁRI, ALBERT BR. DR.: "Rozsnyói gombkötők" [Button-braiders of Rozsnyó]. *Néprajzi Értesítő*, (1904).

NYIRESI-TICHY, KÁLMÁN: *A rozsnyói városi múzeum céhtáblái* [Guild Summoning Tablets in the Rozsnyó Municipal Museum]. Klny. az *Új Magyar Múzeum* III. kötet I(V) füzetéből [Off-print from The New Hungarian Museum Vol. III. brochure I (V)]. Kassa, 1943.

RESCH, ADOLF: "A brassói ötvöscéh bemondó táblája 1556-ból" [The Summoning Tablet of the Brassó Goldsmiths' Guild from 1556]. *Archaeologiai Értesítő*, (1887) pp. 289–293.

ŠERCER, MARIJA: "Zagrebacke cehovske tablice" [Zagreb Guild Tablets]. Posebni otisak iz Zbornika "Iz starog i novog Zagreba IV." Muzej grada Zagreba 1968. pp. 155–170.

ŠPRUSANSKY, SVETOZAR: "Cechové zvolávacie tabulky v zbierach Slovenského Narodného Muzea v Bratislave" [Guild Summoning Boards in the Bratislava Slovak National Museum]. *Annales Musei Nationalis Slovaci Historia* 9. Ročnik LXIII (1969).

SZALAY, EMŐKE: "Debreceni céhbehívótáblák." [Guild Summoning Tablets in Debrecen]. *A debreceni Déri Múzeum Évkönyve* 1977 [Yearbook of the Debrecen Déri Museum.] pp. 201–227.

ZOLTAI, LAJOS: "Czéhládák és egyéb czéhemlékek a debreceni Városi Múzeumban" [Guild Chests and Other Guild Relics in the Debrecen Municipal Museum]. *Néprajzi Értesítő*, (1906). p. 244.

List of Place Names

	Today
Bánffyhunyad	Huedin (Rumania)
Bártfa	Bardejov (Czechoslovakia)
Besztercebánya	Banská Bystrica (Czechoslovakia)
Brassó	Braşov (Rumania)
Dés	Dej (Rumania)
Dobsina	Dobšiná (Czechoslovakia)
Eperjes	Prešov (Czechoslovakia)
Érsekújvár	Nové Zámky (Czechoslovakia)
Fogaras	Făgăraş (Rumania)
Homonna	Humenné (Czechoslovakia)
Igló	Spisská Nová Ves (Czechoslovakia)
Jolsva	Jelšava (Czechoslovakia)
Kassa	Košice (Czechoslovakia)
Késmárk	Kežmarok (Czechoslovakia)
Kézdivásárhely	Tîrgu Secuiesc (Rumania)
Kismarton	Eisenstadt (Austria)
Kisselyk	Şeica-Mică (Rumania)
Kisszeben	Sabinov (Czechoslovakia)
Kolozsvár	Cluj-Napoca (Rumania)
Légrád	Legrad (Jugoslavia)
Léva	Levice (Czechoslovakia)
Liptószentmiklós	Liptovský Sväty Mikuláš (Czechoslovakia)
Lőcse	Levoča (Czechoslovakia)
Losonc	Lučenec (Czechoslovakia)
Marosvásárhely	Tîrgu Mureş (Rumania)
Mateóc	Matejovce (Czechoslovakia)
Munkács	Mukachevo (Soviet Union)
Nagybánya	Baia Mare (Rumania)
Nagyenyed	Aiud (Rumania)
Nagymihály	Michalovce (Czechoslovakia)

Nagyrőce	Vel'ká Revúcá (Czechoslovakia)
Nagysáros	Vel'ký Šariš (Czechoslovakia)
Nagyszeben	Sibiu (Rumania)
Nagyszombat	Trnava (Czechoslovakia)
Nagyvárad	Oradea (Rumania)
Németlipcse	Partizánska Ľupča (Czechoslovakia)
Németpróna	Nitrianske Pravno (Czechoslovakia)
Nyitra	Nitra (Czechoslovakia)
Pelsőc	Plešivec (Czechoslovakia)
Pozsony	Bratislava (Czechoslovakia)
Ratkó	Ratková (Czechoslovakia)
Rimaszombat	Rimavská Sobota (Czechoslovakia)
Rohonc	Rechnitz (Austria)
Rózsahegy	Ružomberok (Czechoslovakia)
Rozsnyó	Rožňava (Czechoslovakia)
Segesvár	Sighişoara (Rumania)
Strázsa	Straža (Chechoslovakia)
Szászrégen	Reghin (Rumania)
Szatmárnémeti	Satu Mare (Rumania)
Székelyudvarhely	Odorhei (Rumania)
Szepesváralja	Spišské Podhradie (Czechoslovakia)
Szepsi	Moldova nad Bodvou (Czechoslovakia)
Szomolnok	Smolník (Czechoslovakia)
Vajdahunyad	Hunedoara (Rumania)
Zágráb	Zagreb (Jugoslavia)
Zilah	Zalău (Rumania)
Zsolna	Žilina (Czechoslovakia)

1. Summoning tablet of the Sárospatak button-braiders' guild (1710). Calvinist Church Collection, Sárospatak

2. Summoning tablet of the Kőszeg
button-braiders' guild (1650/1753). Jurisich Miklós Museum, Kőszeg

3. Badge of the Brassó ▷
goldsmiths' guild
(1556).
Hungarian National
Museum, Budapest

4a–b. Summoning tablet of the Szepsi locksmiths' and gunsmiths' guild (1585). Calvinist Church Collection, Sárospatak

5a–b. Summoning tablet of the Rozsnyó button-braiders' guild (1653). Hungarian National Museum, Budapest

5c–d. Summoning tablet of an unidentified Upper-Hungarian butchers' guild (1689). Hungarian National Museum, Budapest

6. Summoning tablet of the Jolsva weavers' guild (1756). Hungarian National Museum, Budapest

7a–b. Summoning tablet of the Csorna mixed guild (1673/1801).
Ethnographical Museum, Budapest

8a–b. Summoning tablet of the Jászberény tailors' guild (1769). Jász Museum, Jászberény

9. Summoning tablet of the Igló boot-makers' guild (1658). Hungarian National Museum, Budapest

10a. Summoning tablet of the Devecser boot-makers' guild (1670/1844). Bakonyi Museum, Veszprém

10b. Summoning tablet of the Tósokberénd weavers' guild (1791). Ethnographical Museum, Budapest

11a–b. Summoning tablet of the Devecser tailors' guild (1715). Bakonyi Museum, Veszprém

11c–d. Summoning tablet of the Devecser cartwrights' and wetcoopers' guild (1774). Bakonyi Museum, Veszprém

12a–b. Summoning tablet
of the Székesfehérvár boot-makers'
guild (18th century). István király
Museum, Székesfehérvár

13. Summoning tablet
of a Transylvanian tailors' guild
(1636). Hungarian National Museum,
Budapest

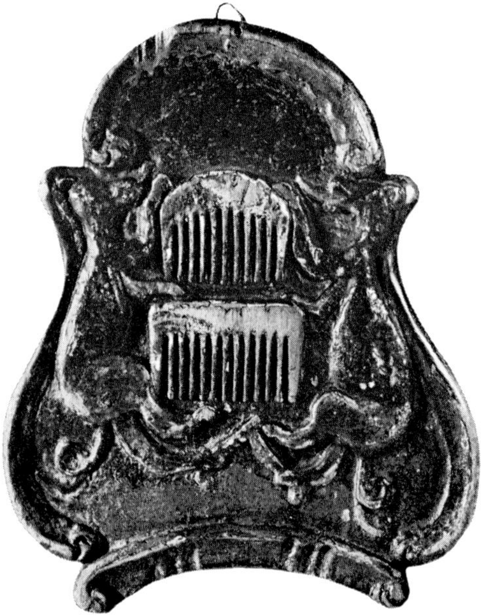

14a—b. Funeral summoning tablet of the Jolsva comb-makers' guild (18th century). Hungarian National Museum, Budapest

15a. Summoning tablet of the Peremarton, Berhida and Kiskovácsi boot-makers' guild (1770). Bakonyi Museum, Veszprém

15b. Summoning tablet of the Szentgál weavers' guild (1801). Bakonyi Museum, Veszprém

SZ GA NE
TA CZ TA
18

16. Summoning tablet of the Debrecen potters' guild (1804).
Déri Museum, Debrecen

17. Summoning tablet of the Gyöngyös harness-makers' guild (1806).
Mátra Museum, Gyöngyös

18. Summoning tablet of the Homonna blacksmiths, locksmiths and bakers' guild (1798). Herman Ottó Museum, Miskolc

19a–b. Summoning tablet
of the Tapolcafő weavers' guild
(1817). Ethnographical Museum,
Budapest

20a. Summoning tablet of the united guild of braziers, turners, needlers, tinsmiths and pewterers of Miskolc (1812). Herman Ottó Museum, Miskolc

20b. Summoning tablet of the Miskolc hatters' guild (1815). Herman Ottó Museum, Miskolc

21. Summoning tablet of the Miskolc cordovan tanners (1855). Herman Ottó Museum, Miskolc

22. Summoning tablet of the Abaújszántó carpenters' and masons' guild (1864). Calvinist Church Collection, Sárospatak

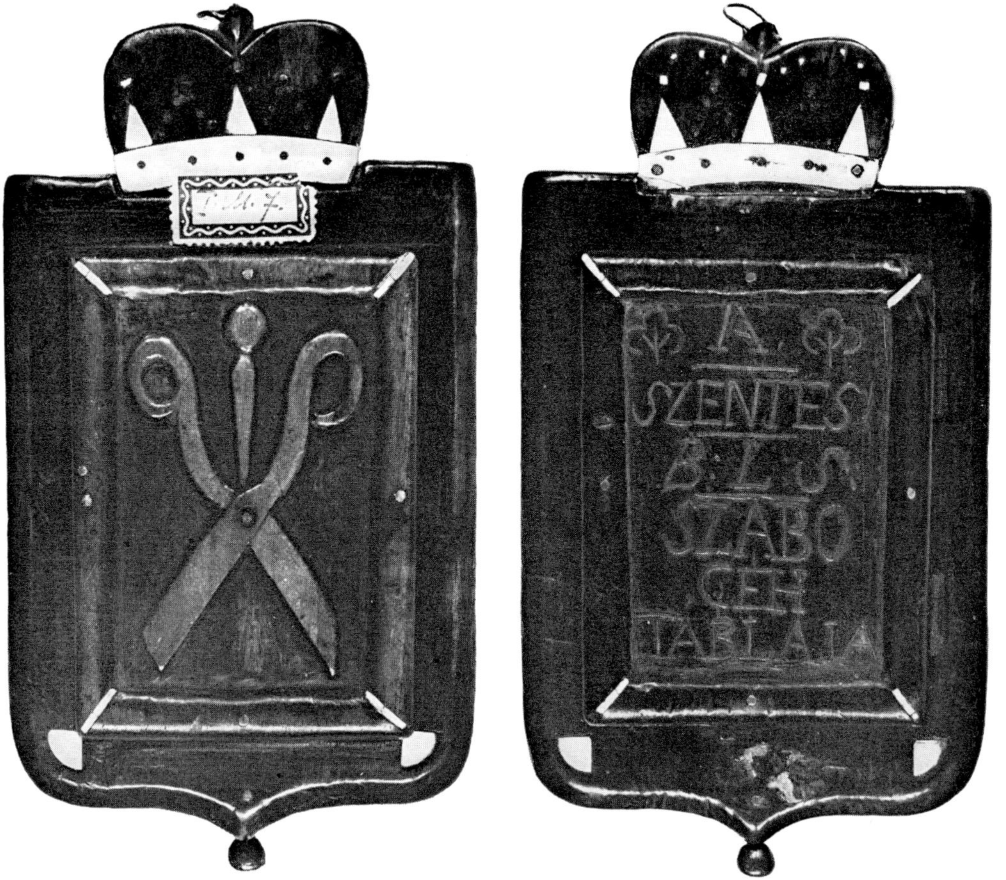

23a–b. Summoning tablet
of the Szentes tailors' guild (1842).
Koszta József Museum, Szentes

24. Summoning tablet of the Veszprém carpenters' guild (19th century). Bakonyi Museum, Veszprém

25a–b. Summoning tablet ▷ of the Pápa potters' guild (1714). Local History Museum, Pápa

PAPAI: NEMES:
FAZEKAS: CEH:
ANNO: 17 14

26a–b. Summoning tablet
of the Veszprém tanners' guild (1800).
Bakonyi Museum, Veszprém

27. Summoning tablet of the Hódmező-vásárhely boot-makers' guild (1754). Tornyai János Museum, Hódmezővásárhely

28a–b. Summoning tablet of button-braiders' guild from Hungary (1651). Museum of Applied Arts, Budapest

29. Summoning tablet of the Debrecen soap-makers' guild (1791). Déri Museum, Debrecen

30a–b. Summoning tablet of a boot-makers' guild from Hungary (end of the 18th century). Hungarian National Museum, Budapest

31. Summoning tablet of the Miskolc locksmiths' guild (1718). Herman Ottó Museum, Miskolc

32a–b. Summoning tablet of the Veszprém gunsmiths' and locksmiths' guild (1725). Bakonyi Museum, Veszprém

33. Summoning tablet of stocking-knitters' guild from Hungary (1725). Museum of Applied Arts, Budapest

34. Summoning tablet
of the Fertőszentmiklós tailors' guild
(1645). Liszt Ferenc Museum, Sopron

35a–b. Summoning tablet of a furriers' guild from Hungary (1817). Ethnographical Museum, Budapest

36a–b. Summoning tablet
of the Vác furriers' guild (1719).
Vak Bottyán Museum, Vác

37a–b. Summoning tablet
of the Székesfehérvár fullers' guild
(18th century). István király Museum,
Székesfehérvár

38a–b. Summoning tablet of the Debrecen butchers' guild (1843). Déri Museum, Debrecen

39. Summoning tablet of an unidentified tanners' guild (early 19th century). Ethnographical Museum, Budapest

40a–b. Summoning tablet of the Buda rope-twisters' guild (1776). Hungarian National Museum, Budapest

41a–b. Summoning tablet of the Szeged bakers' guild (1832). Móra Ferenc Museum, Szeged

42a. Summoning tablet of the Veszprém millers' guild (1797). Bakonyi Museum, Veszprém

42b. Summoning tablet of the Ratkó tanners' guild (18th century). Ethnographical Museum, Budapest

43a–b. Summoning tablet
of the Balassagyarmat boot-makers'
guild (1719). Private collection
of Walter Endrei, Budapest

44. Summoning tablet of an unidentified tailors' guild (1723). Hungarian Labour Movement Museum, Budapest

45. Summoning tablet of the Szomolnok tailors' guild (1759). Hungarian National Museum, Budapest

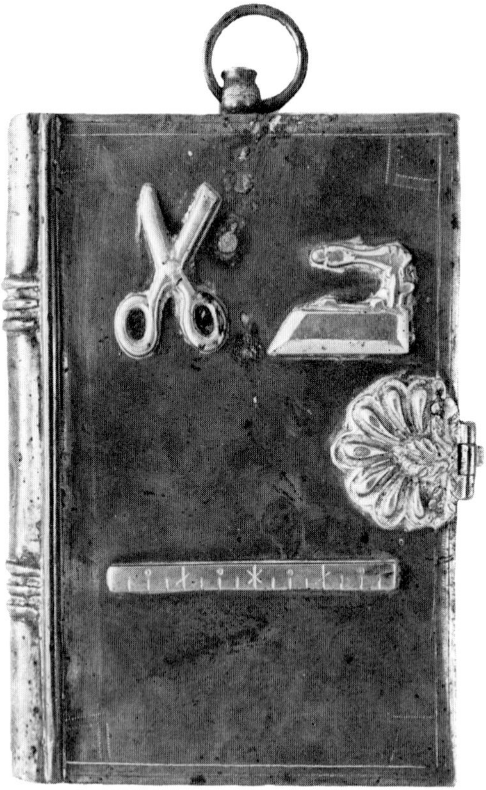

46a. Summoning tablet of the Debrecen *szűr*-tailors' guild (1859). Déri Museum, Debrecen

46b. Summoning tablet of the Miskolc *szűr*-tailors' guild (1869). Herman Ottó Museum, Miskolc

47. Summoning tablet of the Miskolc coopers' guild (1801). Herman Ottó Museum, Miskolc

48. Summoning tablet of the Sopron joiners' guild (1842). Liszt Ferenc Museum, Sopron